Maurine
by Ella Wheeler Wilcox

Copyright © 2019 by HardPress

Address:
HardPress
8345 NW 66TH ST #2561
MIAMI FL 33166-2626
USA
Email: info@hardpress.net

MAURINE.

ELLA WHEELER.

AL 4164.8.74

HARVARD COLLEGE LIBRARY

BOUGHT FROM THE

AMEY RICHMOND SHELDON
FUND

MAURINE.

BY
ELLA WHEELER.
AUTHOR OF "SHELLS," "DROPS OF WATER," &c., &c.

MILWAUKEE:
1876.

HARVARD COLLEGE LIBRARY
SHELDON FUND
JULY 10, 1940

CRAMER, AIKENS & CRAMER,
PUBLISHERS AND PRINTERS,
365 East Water Street,
MILWAUKEE, WIS.

(COPYRIGHTED.)

DEDICATION:

APPRECIATING THE ENCOURAGING SYMPATHY AND KIND
INTEREST MANIFESTED IN THIS WORK

BY

Wm. P. Merrill
AND
Wm. E. Cramer,

IT IS MOST GRATEFULLY DEDICATED TO THEM

BY

THE AUTHOR.

PREFACE.

I'd rather have my verses win
A place in common people's hearts;
Who, toiling through the strife and din
Of life's great thoroughfares and marts,
May read some line my hand has penned;
Some simple verse, not fine, or grand,
But what their hearts can understand,
And hold me henceforth as a friend—
I'd rather win such quiet fame,
Than by some fine thought, polished so
But those of learn-ed minds would know
Just what the meaning of my song,
To have the critics sound my name
In high-flown phrases, loud and long.
I sing not for the critics ear,
But for the masses. If they hear
Despite the turmoil, din, and strife,
Some least low note that gladdens life,
I shall be wholly satisfied,
Though critics to the end deride.

E. W.

INDEX.

		Page
MAURINE,	Part First,	9
"	Part Second,	21
"	Part Third,	36
"	Part Fourth,	56
"	Part Fifth,	78
"	Part Sixth,	99
"	Part Seventh,	116
SOUL OF AMERICA,		142
THE GOSSIPS,		151
MOTHER LOSS,		154
NOW THE DAYS ARE GROWING LONGER,		156
ALL THE WORLD,		157
RIVER AND SEA,		159
THE COMMON PEOPLE,		160
OUR BLESSINGS,		163
A FRAGMENT,		164
MISJUDGED,		165
THE MANIAC,		167
THE CHANGE,		169
RELICS,		171
THE DREAMER,		173
NORINE,		174
FLOWN AWAY,		177
THE WORLD,		179
A POEM,		181
LOST,		184
UPON THE WAY,		187
MY VISION,		188
RESIGNED,		190
TWO JUNES,		192
BLESS THE BABIES,		194
SLANDER,		196
THE VOLUPTUARY,		197
PRINCE OF THE WALTZERS,		199
AN OLD MAN'S VIEW,		201
DYING YEAR,		203
PLEA TO SCIENCE,		205
TWO SEASONS,		207
QUESTIONING,		209
THE CHERUB YEAR,		211
SWEETHEART,		212
MY LADY,		215
THE BELLE OF THE SEASON,		217
THREE AND ONE,		219
THROUGH TEARS,		221
MYSELF,		223

MAURINE.

Part First.

I sat and sewed, and sang some tender tune.
O, beauteous was that morn in early June!
Mellow with sunlight, and with blossoms fair:
The climbing rose-tree grew about me there,
And checked with shade the sunny portico
Where, morns like this, I came to read, or sew.

I heard the gate click, and a firm quick tread
Upon the walk. No need to turn my head;
I would mistake, and doubt my own voice sounding,
Before *his* step upon the gravel bounding.
In an unstudied attitude of grace,
He stretched his comely form; and from his face
He tossed the dark, damp curls, and loosed his collar,
Baring his full, grand neck, for winds to kiss,
With one white perfect hand. Alone by this
You'd mark him as a poet and a scholar.
There, leaning on his elbow, at my knees,

With his broad hat he fanned the lazy breeze,
And turned his head, and lifted his large eyes,
Of that strange hue we see in ocean dyes,
And call it blue sometimes, and sometimes green,
And save in poet-eyes, not elsewhere seen.

"Lest I should meet with my fair lady's scorning,
For calling quite so early in the morning,
I've brought a passport that can never fail,"
He said, and, laughing, laid the morning mail
Upon my lap. "I'm welcome? so I thought!
I'll figure by the letters that I brought
How glad you are to see me. Only one?
And that one from a lady? I'm undone!
That, lightly skimmed, you'll think me *such* a bore,
And wonder why I did not bring you four.
It's ever thus: a woman can not get
So many letters that she will not fret
O'er one that did not come."
                      "I'll prove you wrong,"
I answered gayly, "here upon the spot!
This little letter, precious if not long,
Is just the one, of all you might have brought,
To please me. You have heard me speak, I'm sure,
Of Helen Trevor: she writes here to say
She's coming out to see me; and will stay
Till Autumn, maybe. She is, like her note,
Petite and dainty, tender, loving, pure.
You'd know her, by a letter that she wrote,

MAURINE.

For a sweet tinted thing. 'Tis alway so :—
Letters all blots, though finely written, show
A slovenly person. Letters stiff, and white
Bespeak a nature, honest, plain, upright.
And tissuey, tinted, perfumed notes, like this,
Tell of a creature formed to pet, and kiss."

My list'ner heard me with a slow, odd smile ;
Stretched in abandon at my feet, the while,
He fanned me idly with his broad-brimmed hat.
" Then all young ladies must be formed for that ! "
He laughed, and said.
                    " Their letters read, and look,
As like as twenty copies of one book.
They're written in a dainty, spider scrawl,
To 'darling, precious Kate,' or 'Fan,' or 'Moll.'
The 'dearest, sweetest' friend they ever had.
They say they 'want to see you, oh so bad ! '
Vow they'll 'forget you, never, *never*, oh ! '
And then they tell about a splendid beau—
A lovely hat—a charming dress, and send
A little scrap of this to every friend.
And then to close, for lack of something better,
They beg you'll 'read and burn this horrid letter.' "

He watched me, smiling. He was prone to vex
And hector me with flings upon my sex.
He liked, he said, to have me flash, and frown ;

So he could tease me, and then laugh me down.
My storms of wrath amused him very much:
He liked to see me go off at a touch;
Anger became me—made my color rise,
And gave an added lustre to my eyes.
So he would talk—and so he watched me now,
To see the hot flush mantle cheek and brow.

Instead, I answered coolly, with a smile,
Felling a seam with utmost care, meanwhile,
"The caustic tongue of Vivian Dangerfield
Is barbed, as ever, for my sex, this morn.
Still unconvinced, no smallest point I yield.
Woman I love, and trust, despite your scorn.
There is some truth in what you say? Well, yes!
Your statements usually hold more or less.
Some women write weak letters—(some men do;)
Some make professions, knowing them untrue.
And woman's friendship, in the time of need,
I own, too often proves a broken reed.
But I believe, and ever will contend,
Woman can be a sister woman's friend,
Giving from out her large heart's bounteous store
A living love—claiming to do no more
Than, through and by that love, she knows she can
And living by her professions, *like a man*.
And such a tie, true friendship's silken tether,
Binds Helen Trevor's heart and mine together.
I love her for her beauty, meekness, grace;

For her white lily soul and angel face.
She loves me, for my greater strength, may be;
Loves—and would give her heart's best blood for me.
And I, to save her from a pain, or cross,
Would suffer any sacrifice or loss.
Such can be woman's friendship for another.
Could man give more, or ask more from a brother?"

I paused: and Vivian leaned his massive head
Against the pillar of the portico,
Smiled his slow, skeptic smile, then laughed, and said:
"Nay, surely not—if what you say be so.
You've made a statement, but no proof's at hand.
Wait—do not flash your eyes so! Understand
I think you quite sincere in all you say:
You love your friend, and she loves you, to-day;
But friendship is not friendship at the best
Till circumstances put it to the test.
Man's, less demonstrative, stands strain and tear,
While woman's, half profession, fails to wear.
Two women love each other passing well—
Say Helen Trevor and Maurine La Pelle,
Just for example.
    Let them daily meet
At ball and concert, in the church and street,
They kiss and coo—they visit, chat, caress;
Their love increases, rather than grows less;
And all goes well, till 'Helen, dear' discovers
That 'Maurine, darling' wins too many lovers.

And then her 'precious friend,' her 'pet,' her 'sweet,'
Becomes a 'minx,' a 'creature all deceit.'
Let Helen smile too oft on Maurine's beaux,
Or wear more stylish or becoming clothes,
Or sport a hat that has a longer feather—
And lo! the strain has broken 'friendship's tether.'
Maurine's sweet smile becomes a frown or pout;
'She's just begun to find that Helen out.'
The breach grows wider—anger fills each heart;
They drift asunder, whom 'but death could part.'
You shake your head? Oh, well, we'll never know!
It is not likely Fate will test you so.
You'll live, and love; and, meeting twice a year,
While life shall last, you'll hold each other dear.
I pray it may be so; it were not best
To shake your faith in woman by the test.
Keep your belief, and nurse it while you can.
I've faith in woman's friendship too—for man!
They're true as steel, as mothers, friends, and wives:
And that's enough to bless us all our lives.
That man's a selfish fellow, and a bore,
Who is unsatisfied, and asks for more."

"But there is need of more!" I here broke in.
"I hold that woman guilty of a sin,
Who would not cling to, and defend another,
As nobly as she would stand by a brother.
Who would not suffer for a sister's sake,
And, were there need to prove her friendship, make

'Most any sacrifice, nor count the cost.
Who would not do this for a friend is lost
To every nobler principle."
                            "Shame, shame!"
Cried Vivian, laughing, "for you now defame
The whole sweet sex; since there's not one would do
The thing you name, nor would I want her to.
I love the sex. My mother was a woman—
I hope my wife will be, and wholly human.
And if she wants to make some sacrifice,
I'll think her far more sensible and wise
To let her husband reap the benefit,
Instead of some old maid or senseless chit.
Selfish? Of course! I hold all love is so:
And I shall love my wife right well, I know.
Now there's a point regarding selfish love,
You thirst to argue with me, and disprove.
But since these cosy hours will soon be gone,
And all our meetings broken in·upon,
No more of these rare moments must be spent
In vain discussion, or in argument.
I wish Miss Trevor was in—Jericho!
(You see the selfishness begins to show.)
She wants to see you?—So do I: but she
Will gain her wish, by taking you from me.
'Come all the same?' that means I'll be allowed
To realize that *three* can make a crowd.
I do not like to feel myself *de trop*.
With two girl cronies would I not be so?
My ring would interrupt some private chat.

You'd ask me in, and take my cane and hat,
And speak about the lovely summer day,
And think—'The lout! I wish he'd kept away.'
Miss Trevor 'd smile, but just to hide a pout,
And count the moments till I was shown out.
And, while I twirled my thumbs, I should sit wishing
That I had gone off hunting birds, or fishing.
No, thanks Maurine ! The iron hand of Fate,
(Or otherwise Miss Trevor's dainty fingers,)
Will bar my entrance into Eden's gate ;
And I shall be like some poor soul that lingers
At heaven's portal, paying the price of sin,
Yet hoping to be pardoned and let in."

He looked so melancholy sitting there,
I laughed outright. "How well you act a part ;
You look the very picture of despair !
You've missed your calling, sir ! suppose you start
Upon a starring tour, and carve your name
With Booth's and Forrest's on the heights of Fame.
But now, tabooing nonsense, I shall send
For you to help me entertain my friend,
Unless you come without it. 'Cronies'? True,
Wanting our 'private chats' as cronies do.
And we'll take those, while you are reading Greek,
Or writing 'Lines to Dora's brow,' or 'cheek.'
But when you have an hour or two of leisure,
Call as you now do, and afford like pleasure.
For never yet did heaven's sun shine on,

MAURINE.

Or stars discover, that phenomenon,
In any country, or in any clime:
Two maids so bound, by ties of mind and heart,
They did not feel the heavy weight of time
In weeks of scenes wherein no man took part.
God made the sexes to associate:
Nor law of man, nor stern decree of Fate,
Can ever undo what His hand has done,
And, quite alone, make happy either one.
My Helen is an only child:—a pet
Of loving parents: and she never yet
Has been denied one boon for which she pleaded.
A fragile thing, her lightest wish was heeded.
Would she pluck roses? they must first be shorn
By careful hands, of every hateful thorn.
And loving eyes must scan the pathway where
Her feet may tread, to see no stones are there.
She'll grow dull here, in this secluded nook,
Unless you aid me in the pleasant task
Of entertaining. Drop in with your book—
Read, talk, sing for her sometimes. What I ask,
Do once, to please me: then there'll be no need
For me to state the case again, or plead.
There's nothing like a woman's grace and beauty
To waken mankind to a sense of duty."

"I bow before the mandate of my queen:
Your slightest wish is law, Ma Belle Maurine,"
He answered smiling. "I'm at your command;

Point but one lily finger, or your wand,
And you will find a willing slave obeying.
There goes my dinner bell! I hear it saying
I've spent two hours here, lying at your feet,
Not profitable, may be—surely sweet.
All time is money: now were I to measure
The time I spend here by its solid pleasure,
And that were coined in dollars,—then I've laid
Each day a fortune at your feet, fair maid.
There goes that bell again! I'll say good-bye,
Or clouds will shadow my domestic sky.
Nothing will try a woman's temper, quite,
Like trespassing upon her appetite.
I'll come again, as you would have me do,
And see your friend, while she is seeing you.
That's like by proxy being at a feast;
Unsatisfactory, to say the least."

He drew his fine shape up, and trod the land
With kingly grace. Passing the gate, his hand
He lightly placed the garden wall upon,
Leaped over like a leopard, and was gone.

And, going, took some brightness from the place,
Yet left the June day with a sweeter grace,
And my young soul so steeped in happy dreams,
Heaven itself seemed shown to me in gleams.

There is a time, with lovers, when the heart
First slowly rouses from its dreamless sleep,
To all the tumult of a passion life,
Ere yet have wakened jealousy and strife.
Just as a young, untutored child will start
Out of a long hour's slumber, sound and deep,
And lie and smile with rosy lips, and cheeks,
In a sweet trance, before it stirs or speaks.
A time when yet no word the spell has broken,
Save what the heart unto the soul has spoken,
In quickened throbs, and sighs but half suppressed.
A time when that sweet truth, all unconfessed,
Gives added fragrance to the summer flowers,
A golden glory to the passing hours,
A hopeful beauty to the plainest face,
And lends to life a new and tender grace.

When the full heart has climbed the heights of bliss,
And, smiling, looks back o'er the golden past,
I think it finds no sweeter hour than this
In all love-life. For, later, when the last
Translucent drop o'erflows the cup of joy,
And love, more mighty than the heart's control,
Surges in words of passion from the soul,
And vows are asked and given,—shadows rise
Like mists before the sun in noonday skies,
Vague fears, that prove the brimming cup's alloy :—
A dread of change—the crowning moment's curse,
Since what is perfect, change but renders worse :

A vain desire to cripple Time, who goes
Bearing our joys away, and bringing woes.
And later, doubts and jealousies awaken,
And plighted hearts are tempest-tossed, and shaken.
Doubt sends a test, that goes a step too far,
A wound is made, that, healing, leaves a scar,
Or, one heart, full with love's sweet satisfaction,
Thinks truth once spoken, always understood,
While one is pining for the tender action
And whispered word by which, of old, 'twas wooed.

But this blest hour, in love's glad, golden day,
Is like the dawning, ere the radiant ray
Of glowing Sol has burst upon the eye,
But yet is heralded in earth and sky,
Warm with its fervor, mellow with its light,
While Care still slumbers in the arms of night.
But Hope, awake, hears happy birdlings sing,
And thinks of all a summer day may bring.

In this sweet calm, my young heart lay at rest,
Filled with a blissful sense of peace; nor guessed
That sullen clouds were gathering in the skies
To hide the glorious sun, ere it should rise.

Part Second.

To little birds that never tire of humming
About the garden, in the summer weather,
Aunt Ruth compared us, after Helen's coming,
As we two roamed, or sat and talked together.
Twelve months apart, we had so much to say
Of school days gone—and time since passed away;
Of that old friend, and this; of what we'd done;
Of how our separate paths in life had run;
Of what we would do, in the coming years;
Of plans and castles, hopes and dreams and fears.
All this, and more, as soon as we found speech,
We touched upon, and skimmed from this to that.
But at the first, each only gazed on each,
And, dumb with joy, that did not need a voice
Like lesser joys, to say, "Lo! I rejoice,"
With smiling eyes and clasping hands, we sat
Wrapped in that peace, felt but with those most dear,
Contented just to know each other near.
But when this silent eloquence gave place
To words, 'twas like the rising of a flood
Above a dam. We sat there, face to face,
And let our tongues run on whate'er seemed good,
Speech never halting in its speed or zest,

Save when our rippling laughter let it rest:
Just as a stream will sometimes pause, and play
About a bubbling spring, then dash away.
No wonder, then, the third day's sun was nigh
Up to the zenith when my friend and I
Opened our eyes from slumber long and deep:
Nature demanding recompense for hours
Spent in the portico, among the flowers.
Halves of two nights we should have spent in sleep.

So this third day, we breakfasted at one:
Then walked about the garden in the sun,
Hearing the thrushes and the robins sing,
And looking to see what buds were opening.
Maidens delight in probing a flower's heart,
And finding the hidden beauty of the whole,
Just as they like, by skillful tact and art,
To find the secret of some sister's soul.
'Tis woman-nature! her first query, "Why?"
To answer which, she uses her quick eye.
Why is one rose more drooping than the rest?
She looks, and finds a worm gnaws at its breast.
Why one so red? No reason she can see,
Unless because it's favorite of the bee.
And so she finds, through logic, skill and tact,
Some reason for each sister's mood and act.
Used as she uses it, among her bowers,
Casting the worms out, lifting pallid flowers—
Giving them light and moisture,—not revealing

What sweet, shy secret, red rose is concealing,—
Why, then, this probing but results in good,
And answers the purpose God designed it should.

The clock chimed three, and we yet strayed at will
About the yard in morning dishabille,
When Aunt Ruth came, with apron o'er her head,
Holding a letter in her hand, and said
"Here is a note, from Vivian I opine;
At least his servant brought it. And now girls,
You may think this is no concern of mine,
But in my day young ladies did not go,
Till almost bed-time, roaming to and fro
In morning wrappers, and with tangled curls,
The very pictures of forlorn distress.
'Tis three o'clock, and time for you to dress.
Come! read your note and hurry in, Maurine,
And make yourself fit object to be seen."

Helen was bending o'er an almond bush,
And ere she looked up I had read the note,
And calmed my heart, that, bounding, sent a flush
To brow and cheek, at sight of aught *he* wrote.
"Ma Belle Maurine:" (so Vivian's billet ran,)
"Isn't it time I saw your cherished guest?
'Pity the sorrows of a poor young man'
Banished from all that makes existence blest.
I'm dying to see—your friend; and I will come

And pay respects, hoping you'll be at home
To-night at seven. Expectantly, V. D."

Inside my belt I slipped the billet, saying,
"Helen, go make yourself most fair to see:
Quick! hurry now! no time for more delaying!
In just four hours a caller will be here,
And you must look your prettiest, my dear!
Begin your toilet right away. I know
How long it takes you to arrange each bow—
To twist each curl, and loop your skirts aright.
And you must prove you are *au fait* to-night,
And make a perfect toilet: for our caller
Is man, and critic, poet, artist, scholar,
And views with eyes of all."
       "Oh, oh! Maurine!"
Cried Helen with a well-feigned look of fear,
"You've frightened me so I shall not appear:
I'll hide away, refusing to be seen
By such an ogre. Woe is me! bereft
Of all my friends, my peaceful home I've left,
And strayed away into the dreadful wood
To meet the fate of poor Red Riding Hood.
No, Maurine, no! you've given me such a fright,
I'll not go near your ugly wolf to-night."

Meantime we'd left the garden; and I stood
In Helen's room, where she had thrown herself

Upon a couch, and lay, a winsome elf,
Pouting and smiling, cheek upon her arm,
Not in the least a portrait of alarm.
"Now sweet!" I coaxed, kneeling by her, "be good!
Go curl your hair; and please your own Maurine,
By putting on that lovely grenadine.
Not wolf, nor ogre, neither Caliban,
Nor Mephistopheles, you'll meet to-night,
But what the ladies call 'a nice young man'!
Yet one worth knowing—strong with health and might
Of perfect manhood; gifted, noble, wise;
Moving among his kind with loving eyes,
And helpful hand; progressive, brave, refined,
After the image of his Maker's mind."

"Now, now, Maurine!" cried Helen, "I believe
It is your lover coming here this eve.
Why have you never written of him? pray!
Is the day set?—and when? Say, Maurine, say!"

Had I betrayed by some too fervent word
The secret love that all my being stirred?
My lover? Ay! My heart proclaimed him so;
But first *his* lips must win the sweet confession,
Ere even Helen be allowed to know,
I must straightway erase the slight impression.
Made by the words just uttered.

c

"Foolish child!"
I gayly cried, "your fancy's straying wild.
Just let a girl of eighteen hear the name
Of maid and youth uttered about one time,
And off her fancy goes, at break-neck pace,
Defying circumstances, reason, space—
And straightway builds a romance so sublime
It puts all Shakespeare's dramas to the shame.
This Vivian Dangerfield is neighbor, friend
And kind companion; bringing books and flowers,
And, by his thoughtful actions without end,
Helping me pass some otherwise long hours;
But he has never breathed a word of love.
If you still doubt me, listen while I prove
My statement by the letter that he wrote.
'Dying to meet—my friend?' (she could not see
The dash between that meant so much to me.)
'Will come this eve, at seven; hopes we may
Be in to greet him.' Now I think you'll say
'Tis not much like a lover's tender note.
There—go and 'fix'; and look your prettiest.
A first impression's everything. Put on
The dress I spoke of. I? Oh, I will don—
I don't know what! The first thing that I touch
There in my wardrobe. It won't matter much,
For Vivian's seen me at my worst, and best."

We laugh, we jest, not meaning what we say;
We hide our thoughts, by light words lightly spoken,

And pass on heedless, till we find one day
They've bruised our hearts, and left some other broken.

I sought my room, trilling some merry air;
Opened my wardrobe, wond'ring what to wear.
Momentous question! femininely human!
More than all others, vexing mind of woman,
Since Eve first plucked the fig leaves, hesitating
Before she used them—mentally debating
Whether palm leaves would not be more becoming.
So at my wardrobe, I stood, lightly humming,
All undecided what I should put on.
At length I made selection of a lawn—
White, with a tiny pink vine overrun :—
My simplest robe, but Vivian's favorite one.
Girding it with a ribbon-belt of rose,
And placing a single flowret in my hair,
I crossed the hall to Helen's chamber, where
I found her overhauling all her clothes,
Seeking the robe she wanted.
     "What! all dressed?"
She cried, "I see you're just as spry as ever.
Now, Maurine, tell me why it is I never
Can find my things right handily like you.
I've lost my dress! you needn't laugh, it's true!
Oh! here it is, hanging behind the rest.
Now find my skirts, please, while I loop my curls,
And I will call you just the best of girls."

'Twas like a picture, or a pleasing play,
To watch her make her toilet. She would stand,
And turn her head first this, and then that way,
Trying effect of ribbon, bow or band.
Then she would pick up something else, and curve
Her pretty neck, with cunning, bird-like grace,
And watch the mirror while she put it on,
With such a sweetly grave and thoughtful face;
And then to view it all would sway, and swerve
Her lithe young body, like a graceful swan.

Helen was over medium height, and slender
Even to frailty. Her large, wistful eyes
Were like the deep blue of autumnal skies;
And through them looked her soul, large, loving, tender.
Her long, light hair was lusterless, except
Upon the ends, where burnished sunbeams slept,
And on the ear-locks; and she looped the curls
Back with a shell comb, studded thick with pearls,
Costly yet simple. Her pale loveliness,
That night, was heightened by her rich, black dress,
That trailed behind her, leaving half in sight
Her taper arms, and shoulders marble white.

I was not tall as Helen, and my face
Had the full contour of my grandsire's race;
For through his veins my own received the warm,

Red blood of France, which rounded out my form,
And glowed upon my cheek in crimson dyes,
And bronzed my hair, and darkled in my eyes.
And as the morning, trailing the skirts of night,
And dusky night, stealing the garb of morn,
Go hand in hand what time the day is born,
So we two glided down the hall and stair,
Arm clasping arm, into the parlor, where
Sat Vivian, bathed in sunset's gorgeous light.
He rose to greet us. Oh! his form was grand;
And he possessed that power, strange, occult,
Called magnetism, lacking better word,
Which moves the world, achieving great result
Where genius fails completely. Touch his hand,
It thrilled through all your being—meet his eye,
And you were moved, yet knew not how, or why.
Let him but rise, you felt the air was stirred
By an electric current.
     This strange force
Is mightier than genius. Rightly used,
It leads to grand achievements; all things yield
Before its mystic presence, and its field
Is broad as earth and heaven. But abused,
It sweeps like a poison simoon on its course,
Bearing miasma in its scorching breath,
And leaving all it touches struck with death.

Far-reaching Science shall yet tear away
The mystic garb that hides it from the day,

And drag it forth, and bind it with its laws,
And make it serve the purposes of men,
Guided by common sense and reason. Then
We'll hear no more of seance, table-rapping,
And all that trash, o'er which the world is gaping,
Lost in effect, while Science seeks the cause.

Vivian was not conscious of his power:
Or, if he was, knew not its full extent.
He knew his glance would make a wild beast cower,
And yet he knew not that his large eyes sent
Into the heart of woman the same thrill
That made the lion servant of his will.
And even strong men felt it.
                              He arose,
Reached forth his hand, and, in it, clasped my own,
While I held Helen's; and he spoke some word
Of pleasant greeting in his low, round tone,
Unlike all other voices I have heard.
Just as the white cloud, at the sunrise, glows
With roseate colors, so the pallid hue
Of Helen's cheek, like tinted sea-shells grew.
Through mine, his hand caused hers to tremble: such
Was the all-mast'ring magic of his touch.

Then we sat down, and talked about the weather,
The neighborhood—some author's last new book.

MAURINE.

But, when I could, I left the two together
To make acquaintance, saying, I must look
After the chickens—my especial care;
And ran away, and left them, laughing, there.

Knee-deep, through clover, to the poplar grove,
I waded, where my pets were wont to rove:
And there I found the foolish mother hen
Brooding her chickens underneath a tree,
An easy prey for foxes. "Chick a dee,"
Quoth I, while reaching for the downy things
That, chirping, peeped from out the mother-wings,
"How very human is your folly! When
There waits a haven, pleasant, bright, and warm,
And one to lead you thither from the storm
And lurking dangers, yet you turn away,
And, thinking to be your own protector, stray
Into the open jaws of death: for, see!
An owl is sitting in this véry tree
You thought safe shelter. Go now to your pen."
And, followed by the clucking, clam'rous hen,
So like the human mother here again,
Moaning because a strong, protecting arm
Shielded her little ones from cold and harm,
I carried back my garden hat brim full
Of chirping chickens, like white balls of wool,
And snugly housed them.
                   And just then I heard
A sound like gentle winds among the trees,

Or pleasant waters, in the Summer, stirred
And set in motion by a passing breeze.
'Twas Helen singing: and, as I drew near,
Another voice, a tenor full and clear,
Mingled with hers, as murmuring streams unite,
And flow on stronger in their wedded might.

It was a way of Helen's, not to sing
The songs that other people sang. She took
Sometimes an extract from an ancient book;
Again some floating, fragmentary thing,
And such she fitted to old melodies,
Or else composed the music. One of these
She sang that night; and Vivian caught the strain,
And joined her in the chorus, or refrain.

SONG.

O thou, mine other, stronger part!
  Whom yet I cannot hear, or see,
Come thou, and take this loving heart,
  That longs to yield its all to thee.
I call mine own—Oh come to me!
  Love, answer back, I come to thee,
              I come to thee.

This hungry heart, so warm, so large,
  Is far too great a care for me.
I have grown weary of the charge

I keep so sacredly for thee.
Come thou, and take my heart from me.
Love, answer back, I come to thee,
                    I come to thee.

I am aweary, waiting here
  For one who tarries long from me.
O! art thou far, or art thou near?
And must I still be sad for thee?
Or wilt thou straightway come to me?
Love, answer, I am near to thee,
                    I come to thee.

The melody, so full of plaintive chords,
Sobbed into silence,—echoing down the strings
Like voice of one who walks from us, and sings.
Vivian had leaned upon the instrument
The while they sang. But, as he spoke those words,
"Love, I am near to thee, I come to thee,"
He turned his grand head slowly round, and bent
His lustrous, soulful, speaking gaze on me.
And my young heart, eager to own its king,
Sent to my eyes a great, glad, trustful light,
Of love and faith, and hung upon my cheek
Hope's rose-hued flag. There was no need to speak.
I crossed the room, and knelt by Helen. "Sing
That song you sang a little of one night,
Out on the porch, beginning 'Praise me not,'"
I whispered: and her sweet and plaintive tone
Rose, low and tender, as if she had caught
From some sad passing breeze, and made her own,

The echo of the wind-harp's sighing strain,
Or the soft music of the falling rain.

SONG.

O praise me not with your lips, dear one!
　Though your tender words I prize.
But dearer by far is the soulful gaze,
　Of your eyes, your beautiful eyes,
　　　Your tender, loving eyes.

O chide me not with your lips, dear one!
　Though I cause your bosom sighs.
You can make repentance deeper far
　By your sad, reproving eyes,
　　　Your sorrowful, troubled eyes.

Words, at the best, are but hollow sounds;
　Above, in the beaming skies,
The constant stars say never a word,
　But only smile with their eyes—
　　　Smile on with their lustrous eyes.

Then breathe no vow with your lips, dear one;
　On the wing-ed wind, speech flies.
But I read the truth of your noble heart
　In your soulful, speaking eyes—
　　　In your deep and beautiful eyes.

The twilight darkened 'round us, in the room,
While Helen sang ; and, in the gath'ring gloom,
Vivian reached out, and took my hand in his,

And held it so ; while Helen made the air
Languid with music. Then a step drew near,
And voice of Aunt Ruth broke the spell ;
                            "Dear ! dear !
Why Maurie, Helen, children ! how is this?
I hear you, but you have no light in there.
Your room is dark as Egypt. What a way
For folks to visit !—Maurie, go, I pray,
And order lamps."
                    And so there came a light,
And all the sweet dreams hovering 'round
The twilight shadows flitted in affright :
And e'en the music had a harsher sound.

In pleasant converse passed an hour away :
And Vivian planned a picnic for next day—
A drive the next, and rambles without end,
That he might help me entertain my friend.
And then he rose, bowed low, and passed from sight,
Like some great star that drops out from the night ;
And Helen watched him through the shadows go,
And turned and said, her voice subdued and low,
"How tall he is ! in all my life, Maurine,
A grander man I never yet have seen."

Part Third.

One golden twelfth-part, of a checkered year;
One summer month, of sunlight, moonlight, mirth,
With not a hint of shadows lurking near
Or storm clouds brewing.
     'Twas a royal day:
Voluptuous July, held her lover, Earth,
With her warm arms, upon her glowing breast,
And twined herself about him, as he lay
Smiling and panting in his dream-stirred rest.
She bound him with her limbs of perfect grace,
And hid him with her trailing robe of green,
And wound him in her long hair's shimmering sheen,
And rained her ardent kisses on his face.
  Through the glad glory of the summer land
Helen and I went wand'ring, hand in hand.
In winding paths, hard by the ripe wheat field,
White, with the promise of a bounteous yield,
Across the late shorn meadow—down the hill
Red with the tiger-lily blossoms, till
We stood upon the borders of the lake
That like a pretty, placid infant slept
Low at its base: and little ripples crept
Along its surface, just as dimples chase

MAURINE.

Each other, o'er an infant's sleeping face.
    Helen in idle hours had learned to make
A thousand pretty, feminine knick-knacks :
For brackets, ottomans, and toilet stands—
Labor just suited to her dainty hands.
    That morning she had been at work in wax,
Moulding a wreath of flowers for my room,—
Taking her patterns from the living blows
In all their dewy beauty and sweet bloom
Fresh from my garden. Fuchsia, tulip, rose,
And trailing ivy, grew beneath her touch,
Resembling the living plants, as much
As life is copied in the form of death :
These lacking but the perfume, and that, breath.

And now the wreath was all completed, save
The mermaid blossom of all flowerdom,
A water lily, dripping from the wave.
And 'twas in search of it that we had come
Down to the lake, and wandered on the beach
To see if any lilies grew in reach.
Some broken stalks, where flowers late had been ;
Some buds, with all their beauties folded in,
We found, but not the treasure that we sought.
And then we turned our footsteps to the spot
Where all impatient of its chain, my boat
"The Swan" rocked, asking to be set afloat.
It was a dainty row boat—strong yet light ;
Each side a swan was painted snowy white :

A present from my uncle, just before
He sailed, with Death, to that mysterious strand,
Where freighted ships go sailing evermore,
But none return to tell us of the land.
    I freed the "Swan," and slowly rowed about
Wherever sea-weeds, grass, or green leaves lifted
Their tips above the water. So we drifted
While Helen, opposite, leaned idly out
And watched for lilies in the waves below,
And softly crooned some sweet and dreamy air
That soothed me like a mother's lullabies.
I dropped the oars, and closed my sun-kissed eyes,
And let the boat go drifting here and there.
O happy day! the last of that brief time
Of thoughtless youth, when all the world seems bright,
Ere that disguis-ed angel men call Woe
Leads the sad heart through valleys dark as night,
Up to the heights exalted and sublime.
On each blest, happy moment, I am fain
To linger long, ere I pass on to pain
And sorrow that succeeded.
                    From day dreams,
As golden as the summer noon-tide's beams,
I was awakened by a voice that cried,
"Strange ship ahoy! Fair frigate, whither bound?"
And, starting up, I cast my gaze around,
And saw a sail boat o'er the water glide
Close to the "Swan," like some live thing of grace;
And from it looked the glowing, handsome face
Of Vivian.

"Beauteous sirens of the sea,
Come sail across the raging main with me!"
He laughed; and leaning, drew our drifting boat
Beside his own. "There now! step in!" he said,
"I'll land you anywhere you want to go—
My boat is safer far than yours, I know:
And much more pleasant with its sails all spread.
The Swan? We'll take the oars, and let it float
Ashore at leisure. You, Maurine, sit there—
Miss Helen here. Ye gods and little fishes!
I've reached the height of pleasure, and my wishes.
Adieu despondency! farewell to care!
What greater boon could man desire than this—
To skim the waters under balmy skies,
Cheered by soft glances from two Houris' eyes,
Fanned by sweet winds? Oh ecstasy of bliss!"

'Twas done so quickly: that was Vivian's way.
He did not wait for either yea, or nay.
He gave commands, and left you with no choice
But just to do the bidding of his voice.
His rare kind smile, low tones, and manly face
Lent to his quick imperiousness a grace
And winning charm, completely stripping it
Of what might otherwise have seemed unfit.
Leaving no trace of tyranny, but just
That nameless force that seemed to say, "You must."

Suiting its pretty title of "The Dawn,"
(So named, he said, that it might rhyme with "Swan,
Vivian's sail boat, was carpeted with blue,
While all its sails were of a pale rose hue.
The daintiest craft that flirted with the breeze:
A poet's fancy in an hour of ease.

Whatever Vivian had was of the best.
His room was like some Sultan's in the east.
His board was always spread as for a feast,
Whereat, each meal, he was both host and guest.
He would go hungry sooner than he'd dine
At his own table if 'twere illy set.
He so loved things artistic in design—
Order, and beauty, all about him. Yet
So kind he was, if it befell his lot
To dine within the humble peasant's cot,
He made it seem his native soil to be,
And thus displayed the true gentility.

Under the rosy banners of the "Dawn,"
Around the lake we drifted on, and on.
It was a time for dreams, and not for speech.
And so we floated on in silence, each
Weaving the fancies suiting such a day.
Helen leaned idly o'er the sail boat's side,
And dipped her rosy fingers in the tide;
And I, among the cushions half reclined,

Half sat, and watched the fleecy clouds at play,
While Vivian with his blank-book, opposite,
In which he seemed to either sketch or write,
Was lost in inspiration of some kind.

No time, no change, no scene can e'er efface
My mind's impression of that hour, and place:
It stands out like a picture. O'er the years,
Black with their robes of sorrow—veiled with tears,
Lying with all their lengthened shapes between,
Untouched, undimmed, I still behold that scene.
Just as the last of Indian summer days,
Perfect with sunlight, crowned with amber haze,
Followed by dark and desolate December,
Through all the months of winter we remember.

The sun slipped westward. That peculiar change
Which creeps into the air, and speaks of night
While yet the day is full of golden light,
We felt steal o'er us.
                Vivian broke the spell
Of dream-fraught silence, throwing down his book:
"Young ladies, please allow me to arrange
These wraps about your shoulders. I know well
The fickle nature of our atmosphere,—
Her smile swift followed by a frown or tear—
And go prepared for changes. Now you look,
Like—like—oh, where's a pretty simile?

D

Had you a pocket mirror here you'd see
How well my native talent is displayed
In shawling you. Red on the brunette maid;
Blue on the blonde—and quite without design.
(Oh where *is* that comparison of mine!)
Well—like a June rose and a violet
In one bouquet! Will that do for a start?
You know I'm but a novice in the art
Of complimenting. Please do not forget
My maiden effort of this afternoon.
And now I crave your patience, and a boon!
Which is to listen, while I read my rhyme,
A floating fancy of the Summer time.
It's neither witty, wonderful, nor wise.
So listen kindly—but don't criticize:

> If all the ships I have at sea
> Should come a-sailing home to me,
> Ah well! the harbor could not hold
> So many sails as there would be
> If all my ships came in from sea.
>
> If half my ships came home from sea,
> And brought their precious freight to me,
> Ah well! I should have wealth as great
> As any king, who sits in state—
> So rich the treasures that would be
> In half my ships now out at sea.
>
> If just one ship I have at sea
> Should come a-sailing home to me,
> Ah, well! the storm clouds then might frown:

MAURINE.

> For if the others all went down
> Still rich and proud and glad I'd be,
> If that one ship came back to me.
>
> If that one ship went down at sea,
> And all the others came to me,
> Weighed down with gems and wealth untold,
> With glory, honors, riches, gold,
> The poorest soul on earth I'd be
> If that one ship came not to me.
>
> O skies be calm! O winds blow free!
> Blow all my ships safe home to me.
> But if thou sendest some a-wrack!
> To never more come sailing back,
> Send any—all, that skim the sea,
> But bring my love-ship home to me.

Helen was leaning by me, and her head
Rested against my shoulder: as he read,
I stroked her hair, and watched the fleecy skies,
And, when he finished, did not turn my eyes.
I felt too happy and too shy to meet
His gaze just then. I said "'Tis very sweet,
And suits the day; doesn't it, Helen, dear?"
But Helen, voiceless, did not seem to hear.
"'Tis strange," I added, "how you poets sing
So feelingly about the very thing
You care not for! and dress up an ideal
So well, it looks a living, breathing real!
Now, to a listener, your love song seemed
A hearts out-pouring: yet I've heard you say
Almost the opposite; or that you deemed

Position, honor, glory, power, fame,
Gained without loss of conscience or good name,
The things to live for."
                    "Have you? Well, you may"
Laughed Vivian, "but 'twas years—or months ago!
And Solomon says wise men change, you know!
I now speak truth! if she I hold most dear,
Slipped from my life, and no least hope were left,
My heart would find the years more lonely here,
Than if I were of wealth, fame, friends bereft,
And sent an exile to a foreign land."

His voice was low, and measured: as he spoke
New, unknown chords of melody awoke
Within my soul. I felt my heart expand
With that sweet fullness born of love. I turned
To hide the blushes on my cheek that burned,
And leaning over Helen, breathed her name.
She lay so motionless I thought she slept:
But, as I spoke, I saw her eyes unclose,
And o'er her face a sudden glory swept,
And a slight tremor thrilled all through her frame,
"Sweet friend," I said, "your face is full of light:
What were the dreams that made your eyes so bright

She only smiled for answer, and arose
From her reclining posture at my side,
Threw back the clust'ring ringlets from her face

With a quick gesture, full of easy grace,
And, turning, spoke to Vivian. "Will you guide
The boat up near that little clump of green
Off at the right? There's where the lilies grow.
We quite forgot our errand here, Maurine,
And our few moments have grown into hours.
What will Aunt Ruth think of our ling'ring so?
There—that will do—now I can reach the flowers."

"Hark! just hear that!" and Vivian broke forth
 singing
"Row, brother, row." "The six o'clock bell's ringing!
Who ever knew three hours to go so fast
In all the annals of the world, before!
I could have sworn, not over one had passed.
Young ladies, I am forced to go ashore!
I'm loth to name the reason, which has not
As much of romance as this hour and spot.
But truth is truth: our supper tables wait—
Romance must yield to appetite and Fate.
I thank you for the pleasure you have given;
This afternoon has been a glimpse of heaven.
Good night—sweet dreams! and by your gracious
 leave,
I'll pay my compliments to-morrow eve."

A smile, a bow, and he had gone his way:
And, in the waning glory of the day,

Down cool green lanes, and through the length'ning
    shadows,
Silent, we wandered back across the meadows.
The wreath was finished, and adorned my room;
Long afterward, the lilies' copied bloom
Was like a horrid spectre in my sight,
Staring upon me, morning, noon and night.

The sun went down. The sad new moon rose up,
And passed before me, like an empty cup
The Great Unseen brims full of pain or bliss,
And gives His children, saying "drink of this."

A light wind, from the open casement, fanned
My brow and Helen's, as we, hand in hand,
Sat looking out upon the twilight scene,
In dreamy silence. Helen's dark blue eyes,
Like two lost stars that wandered from the skies
Some night adown the meteor's shining track,
And always had been grieving to go back,
Now gazed up, wistfully, at heaven's dome
And seemed to recognize, and long for home.

Her sweet voice broke the silence. "Wish, Maurine,
Before you speak! you know the moon is new,
And any thing you wish for will come true

MAURINE.

Before it wanes. I do believe the sign!
Now tell me your wish, and I'll tell you mine."

I turned and looked up at the slim young moon;
And, with an almost superstitious heart,
I sighed, "O, new moon! help me by thine art
To grow all grace and goodness, and to be
Worthy the love a true heart proffers me."
Then smiling down, I said "Dear one! my boon
I fear is quite too silly or too sweet
For my repeating: so we'll let it stay
Between the moon and me. But if I may
I'll listen now to your wish. Tell me, please!"

All suddenly she nestled at my feet,
And hid her blushing face upon my knees.
Then drew my hand against her glowing cheek,
And, leaning on my breast began to speak,
Half sighing out the words my tortured ear
Reached down to catch, while striving not to hear.

"Can you not guess who 'twas about, Maurine?
Oh my sweet friend! you must ere this have seen
The love I tried to cover from all eyes
And from myself. O, foolish little heart!
As well it might go seeking for some art
Whereby to hide the sun in noon-day skies.

When first the strange sound of his voice I heard,
Looked on his noble face, and touched his hand,
My slumb'ring heart thrilled through and through,
    and stirred
As if to say 'I hear, and understand.'
And day by day mine eyes were blest beholding
The inner beauty of his life, unfolding
In countless words and actions, that portrayed
The noble stuff of which his soul was made.
And more and more I felt my heart upreaching
After the truth, drawn gently by his teaching,
As flowers are drawn by sunlight. And there grew
A strange, shy something in its depths, I knew
At length was love, because it was so sad
And yet so sweet, and made my heart so glad,
Yet seemed to pain me. Then, for very shame,
Lest all should read my secret and its name,
I strove to hide it in my breast away
Where God could see it only. But each day
It seemed to grow within me, and would rise
Like my own soul, and look forth from my eyes,
Defying bonds of silence; and would speak
In its red-lettered language on my cheek
If but his name was uttered. You were kind,
My own Maurine! as you alone could be,
So long the sharer of my heart and mind,
While yet you saw, in seeming not to see.
In all the years we have been friends, my own,
And loved as women very rarely do,
My heart no sorrow and no joy has known

It has not shared at once, in full, with you,
And I so longed to speak to you of this,
When first I felt its mingled pain and bliss;
Yet dared not, lest, you, knowing him, should say,
In pity for my folly—'Lack a-day!
You are undone: because no mortal art
Can win the love of such a lofty heart.'
And so I waited, silent and in pain,
Till I could know I did not love in vain.
And now I know, beyond a doubt or fear.
Did he not say, 'If she I hold most dear
Slipped from my life, and no least hope was left,
My heart would find the years more lonely here,
Than if I were of wealth, fame, friends bereft,
And sent an exile to a foreign land?'
Oh, darling! you must *love* to understand
The joy that thrilled all through me at those words.
It was as if a thousand singing birds
Within my heart broke forth in notes of praise.
I did not look up, but I knew his gaze
Was on my face, and that his eyes must see
The joy I felt almost transfigured me.
He loves me—loves me! so the birds kept singing,
And all my soul with that sweet strain is ringing.
If there were added but one drop of bliss,
No more my cup would hold; and so this eve
I made a wish that I might feel his kiss
Upon my lips, ere you, pale moon, should leave
The stars all by themselves and wanel away,
Too old and weak and tired with care to stay."

Her voice sighed into silence. While she spoke
My heart writhed in me, praying she would cease.—
Each word she uttered falling like a stroke
On my bare soul. And now a hush like death,
Save that 'twas broken by a quick drawn breath,
Fell 'round me, but brought not the hoped-for peace.
For when the lash no longer leaves its blows,
The flesh still quivers, and the blood still flows.

She nestled on my bosom like a child.
And 'neath her head my tortured heart throbbed wild
With pain and pity. She had told her tale—
Her self-deceiving story to the end.
How could I look down on her as she lay
So fair, and sweet, and lily-like, and frail—
A tender blossom on my breast, and say
" Nay, you are wrong—you do mistake, dear friend !
'Tis I am loved, not you." Yet that were truth
And she must know it later.
      Should I speak,
And spread a ghastly pallor o'er the cheek
Flushed now with joy ? And while I, doubting,
  pondered,
She spoke again. "Maurine ! I oft have wondered
Why you and Vivian were not lovers. He
Is all a heart could ask its king to be ;
And you have beauty, intellect and youth.
I think it strange you have not loved each other—
Strange how he could pass by you for another

MAURINE.

Not half so fair or worthy. Yet I know
A loving Father pre-arranged it so.
I think my heart has known him all these years,
And waited for him. And if when he came
It had been as the lover of my friend,
I should have recognized him, all the same,
As my soul-mate, and loved him to the end,
Hiding my grief, and forcing back my tears
Till on my heart, slow dropping, day by day,
Unseen they fell, and wore it all away.
And so a tender Father kept him free,
With all the largeness of his love, for me—
For me, unworthy such a precious gift!
Yet I will bend each effort of my life
To grow in grace and goodness, and to lift
My soul and spirit to his lofty height,
So to deserve that holy name, his wife.
Sweet friend, it fills my whole heart with delight
To breathe its long hid secret in your ear.
Speak, my Maurine, and say you love to hear!"

The while she spoke, my active brain gave rise
To one great thought of mighty sacrifice
And self denial. Oh! it blanched my cheek,
And wrung my soul; and from my heart it drove
All life and feeling. Coward-like, I strove
To send it from me : but I felt it cling
And hold fast on my mind like some live thing ;
And all the Self within me felt its touch

And cried, "No, no! I cannot do so much—
I am not strong enough—there is no call."
And then the voice of Helen bade me speak,
And with a calmness born of nerve, I said,
Scarce knowing what I uttered, "Sweetheart, all
Your joys and sorrows are with mine own wed.
I thank you for your confidence, and pray
I may deserve it always. But, dear one,
Something—perhaps our boat-ride in the sun,
Has set my head to aching. I must go
To bed directly; and you will, I know,
Grant me your pardon, and another day
We'll talk of this together. Now good night,
And angels guard you with their wings of light."

I kissed her lips, and held her on my heart,
And viewed her as I ne'r had done before.
I gazed upon her features o'er and o'er;
Marked her white tender face—her fragile form,
Like some frail plant that withers in the storm;
Saw she was fairer in her new found joy
Than e'er before; and thought, "Can I destroy
God's handiwork, or leave it at the best
A broken harp, while I close clasp my bliss?"
I bent my head and gave her one last kiss,
And sought my room, and found there such relief
As sad hearts feel when first alone with grief.

"The moon went down, slow sailing from my sight,
And left the stars to watch away the night.
O stars, sweet stars, so changeless and serene!
What depths of woe, your pitying eyes have seen!
The proud sun sets, and leaves us with our sorrow,
To grope alone in darkness till the morrow.
The languid moon, e'en if she deigns to rise,
Soon seeks her couch, grown weary of our sighs;
But from the early gloaming till the day
Sends golden liveried heralds forth to say
He comes in might; the patient stars shine on,
Steadfast and faithful, from twilight to dawn.
And, as they shone upon Gethsemane,
And watched the struggle of a God-like soul,
Now from the same far height they shone on me,
And saw the waves of anguish o'er me roll.

The storm had come upon me all unseen:
No sound of thunder fell upon my ear;
No cloud arose to tell me it was near;
But under skies all sunlit, and serene,
I floated with the current of the stream,
And thought life all one golden haloed dream.
When lo! a hurricane, with awful force,
Swept swift upon its devastating course,
Wrecked my frail bark, and cast me on the wave
Where all my hopes had found a sudden grave.
Love makes us blind and selfish: otherwise
I had seen Helen's secret in her eyes;

So used I was to reading every look
In her sweet face, as I would read a book.
But now, made sightless by love's blinding rays,
I had gone on, unseeing, to the end,
Where Pain dispelled the mist of golden haze
That walled me in, and lo! I found my friend
Who journeyed with me—at my very side,
Had been sore wounded to the heart, while I
Both deaf and blind, saw not, nor heard her cry.
And then I sobbed, "O God! I would have died
To save her this." And as I cried in pain,
There leaped forth from the still, white realm of
    Thought
Where Conscience dwells, that unimpassioned spot
As widely different from the heart's domain,
As North from South—the impulse felt before,
And put away; but now it rose once more,
In greater strength, and said "Heart, wouldst thou
    prove
What lips have uttered? Then go lay thy love
On Friendship's altar, as thy offering."
"Nay!" cried my heart, "ask any other thing—
Ask life itself—'twere easier sacrifice.
But ask not love, for that I cannot give."

"But," spoke the voice, "the meanest insect dies,
And is no hero! heroes dare to live
When all that makes life sweet is snatched away."
So with my heart, in converse, till the day

In gold and crimson billows, rose, and broke,
The voice of Conscience, all unwearied spoke.
Love warred with Friendship: heart with Conscience
    fo't,
Hours rolled away, and yet the end was not.
And wily Self, tricked out like tenderness,
Sighed, "think how one, whose life thou wert to bless
Will be cast down, and grope in doubt and fear!
Wouldst thou wound him, to give thy friend relief?
Can wrong make right?"
            "Nay!" Conscience said, "but Pride
And Time can heal the saddest hurts of love.
While Friendship's wounds, gap wide and yet more
    wide,
And bitter fountains of the spirit prove."

At length, exhausted with the wearing strife,
I cast the new found burden of my life
On God's broad breast, and sought that deep repose
That only he who's watched with sorrow knows.

Part Fourth.

"Maurine, Maurine! 'tis ten o'clock! arise,
My pretty sluggard! open those dark eyes,
And see where yonder sun is! Do you know
I made my toilet just four hours ago?"

'Twas Helen's voice: and Helen's gentle kiss
Fell on my cheek. As from a deep abyss,
I drew my weary self from that strange sleep
That rests not, nor refreshes. Scarce awake
Or conscious, yet there seemed a heavy weight
Bound on my breast, as by a cruel Fate.
I knew not why, and yet I longed to weep.
Some dark cloud seemed to hang upon the day;
And, for a moment, in that trance I lay,
When suddenly the truth did o'er me break,
Like some great wave upon a helpless child.
The dull pain in my breast grew like a knife—
The heavy throbbing of my heart grew wild,
And God gave back the burden of the life
He kept what time I slumbered.

"You are ill,"
Cried Helen, "with that blinding headache still!
You look so pale and weary. Now let me
Play nurse, Maurine, and care for you to-day!
And first I'll suit some dainty to your taste,
And bring it to you, with a cup of tea."
And off she ran, not waiting my reply.

But, wanting most the sunshine and the light,
I left my couch, and clothed myself in haste,.
And, kneeling, sent to God an earnest cry
For help and guidance.
                        "Show Thou me the way,
Where duty leads ; for I am blind! my sight
Obscured by self. O, lead my steps aright!
Help me to see the path : and if it may,
Let this cup pass :—and yet Thou heavenly One
Thy will in all things, not mine own, be done."
        Rising, I went upon my way, receiving
The strength prayer gives alway to hearts believing.
I felt that unseen hands were leading me,
And knew the end was peace.
                            "What! are you up?"
Cried Helen, coming with a tray, and cup,
Of tender toast, and fragrant smoking tea.
"You naughty girl! you should have stayed in bed
Until you ate your breakfast, and were better?
I've something hidden for you here—a letter.
But drink your tea before you read it, dear!

'Tis from some distant cousin, Auntie said
And so you need not hurry. Now be good,
And mind your Helen."
                        So, in passive mood,
I laid the still unopened letter near,
And nibbled at my breakfast more to please
My nurse, than any hunger to appease.
Then listlessly I broke the seal and read
The few lines written in a bold free hand :
" New London, Canada. Dear Coz. Maurine !
(In spite of generations stretched between
Our natural right to that most handy claim—
Of cousinship, we'll use it all the same)
I'm coming to see you! honestly, in truth !
I've threatened often—now I mean to act.
You'll find my coming is a stubborn fact.
Keep quiet though, and do not tell Aunt Ruth.
I wonder if she'll know her petted boy
In spite of changes. Look for me until
You see me coming. As of old I'm still
Your faithful friend, and loving cousin, Roy."

So Roy was coming! He and I had played
As boy and girl, and later, youth and maid,
Full half our lives together. He had been,
Like me, an orphan ; and the roof of kin
Gave both kind shelter. Swift years sped away
Ere change was felt : and then one summer day

MAURINE.

A long lost uncle sailed from India's shore—
Made Roy his heir, and he was ours no more.

"He'd write us daily, and we'd see his face
Once every year." Such was his promise given
The morn he left. But now the years were seven
Since last he looked upon the olden place.
He'd been through college, traveled in all lands,
Sailed over seas, and trod the desert sands.
Would write and plan a visit, then, ere long,
Would write again from Egypt or Hong Kong—
Some mission called him thither unforeseen.
So years had passed, till seven lay between
His going, and the coming of this note,
Which I hid in my bosom, and replied
To Aunt Ruth's queries, "What the truant wrote?
By saying he was still upon the wing,
And merely dropped a line, while journeying,
To say he lived: and she was satisfied.

Sometimes it happens, in this world so strange,
A human heart will pass through mortal strife,
And writhe in torture: while the old sweet life,
So full of hope, and beauty, bloom, and grace,
Is slowly strangled by remorseless Pain:
And one stern, cold, relentless, takes its place—
A ghastly, pallid spectre of the slain.
Yet those in daily converse see no change

Nor dream the heart has suffered.
So that day
I passed along toward the troubled way
Stern duty pointed, and no mortal guessed
A mighty conflict had disturbed my breast.

I had resolved to yield up to my friend
The man I loved. Since she, too, loved him so
I saw no other way in honor left.
She was so weak and fragile, once bereft
Of this great hope, that held her with such power,
She would wilt down, like some frost-bitten flower,
And swift untimely death would be the end.
But I was strong: and hardy plants, that grow
In out-door soil, can bear bleak winds that blow
From Arctic lands, whereof a single breath
Would lay the hot-house blossom low in death.

The hours went by, too slow, and yet too fast.
All day I argued with my foolish heart
That bade me play the shrinking coward's part
And hide from pain. And when the day had past
And time for Vivian's call drew near and nearer,
It pleaded, "Wait, until the way seems clearer:
Say you are ill—or busy: keep away
Until you gather greater strength to play
The part you have resolved on."

            "Nay, not so,"
Made answer clear-eyed Reason, " Do you go
And put your resolution to the test.
Resolve, however nobly formed, at best
Is but a still-born babe of Thought, until
It proves existence of its life and will
By sound or action."
                    So when Helen came
And knelt by me, her fair face all aflame
With sudden blushes, whispering, " My sweet!
My heart can hear the music of his feet—
Go down with me to meet him." I arose,
And went with her all calmly, as one goes
To look upon the dear face of the dead.

That eve, I know not what I did, or said.
I was not cold—my manner was not strange:
Perchance I talked more freely than my wont,
But in my speech was naught could give affront;
Yet I conveyed, as only woman can,
That nameless *something*, which bespeaks a change.

'Tis in the power of woman, if she be
Whole-souled and noble, free from coquetry—
Her motives all unselfish, worthy, good,
To make herself and feelings understood
By nameless acts—thus sparing what to man,

However gently answered, causes pain,
The off'ring of his hand and heart in vain.

She can be friendly, unrestrained, and kind,
Assume no airs of pride or arrogance;
But in her voice, her manner, and her glance,
Convey that mystic something, undefined,
Which men fail not to understand and read,
And, when not blind with egotism, heed.
My task was harder. 'Twas the slow undoing
Of long sweet months of unimpeded wooing.
It was to hide and cover and conceal
The truth—assuming, what I did not feel.
It was to dam love's happy singing tide
That blessed me with its hopeful, tuneful tone,
By feigned indiff'rence, till it turned aside,
And changed its channel, leaving me alone
To walk parched plains, and thirst for that sweet
    draught
My lips had tasted, but another quaffed.

It could be done. For no words yet were spoken,—
None to recall—no pledges to be broken.
"He will be grieved, then angry, cold, then cross,"
I reasoned, thinking what would be his part
In this strange drama. "Then because his heart
Feels something lacking, to make good his loss,
He'll turn to Helen: and her gentle grace

And loving acts will win her soon the place
I hold to-day: and like a troubled dream
At length, our past, when he looks back, will seem."

That evening passed with music, chat, and song:
But hours that once had flown on airy wings
Now limped on weary, aching limbs along,
Each moment like some dreaded step that brings
A twinge of pain.   As Vivian rose to go,
Slow bending to me, from his greater height,
He took my hand, and, looking in my eyes,
With tender questioning and pained surprise,
Said "Maurine, you are not yourself to-night!
What is it? Are you ailing?"
                              "Ailing? no,"
I answered laughing lightly, "I am not:
Just see my cheek, sir! is it thin, or pale?
Now tell me, am I looking very frail?"
  "Nay, nay!" he answered, "it can not be *seen*,
The change I speak of—'twas more in your mien:
Preoccupation, or—I know not what!
Miss Helen, am I wrong, or does Maurine
Seem to have something on her mind this eve?"

"She does!" laughed Helen, "and I do believe
I know what 'tis! A letter came to-day
Which she read slyly, and then hid away

Close to her heart, not knowing I was near :
And since she's been as you have seen her here.
See how she blushes! so my random shot
We must believe has struck a tender spot."

Her rippling laughter floated through the room,
And redder yet I felt the hot blood rise,
Then surge away, leaving me pale as death,
Under the dark and swiftly gath'ring gloom
Of Vivian's questioning, accusing eyes,
That searched my soul. I almost shrieked beneath
That stern, fixed gaze ; and stood spell-bound until
He turned with sudden movement, gave his hand
To each in turn, saying " You must not stand
Longer, young ladies, in this open door.
The air is heavy with a cold damp chill.
We shall have rain to-morrow, or before.
Good night."
   He vanished in the darkling shade ;
And so the dreaded evening found an end,
That saw me grasp the conscience-whetted blade,
And strike a blow for honor and for friend.

"How swiftly passed the evening!" Helen sighed.
"How long the hours!" my tortured heart replied.

MAURINE.

Joy, like a child, with lightsome steps doth glide
By Father Time, and, looking in his face,
Cries, snatching blossoms from the fair road side
"I could pluck more, but for thy hurried pace."
The while her elder brother Pain, man grown,
Whose feet are hurt by many a thorn and stone,
Looks to some distant hill top, high and calm,
Where he shall find not only rest, but balm
For all his wounds, and cries in tones of woe,
"O Father Time! why is thy pace so slow?"

Two days, all sad with lonely wind and rain,
Went sobbing by, repeating o'er and o'er
The miserere, desolate and drear,
Which every human heart must sometime hear.
Pain is but little varied. Its refrain,
What'er the words are, is for aye the same.
The third day brought a change: for with it came
Not only sunny smiles to Nature's face,
But Roy—our Roy came back to us. Once more
We looked into his laughing, handsome eyes,
Which, while they gave Aunt Ruth a glad surprise
In no way puzzled her: for one glance told
What each succeeding one confirmed, that he
Who bent above her with the lissome grace
Of his fine form, though grown so tall, could be
No other than the Roy Montaine of old.

It was a sweet reunion : and he brought
So much of sunshine with him, that I caught,
Just from his smile alone, enough of gladness
To make my heart forget a time its sadness.
We talked together of the dear old days :
Leaving the present, with its depths and heights
Of life's maturer sorrows and delights,
I turned back to my childhood's level land,
And Roy and I, dear playmates, hand in hand,
Wandered in mem'ry, through the olden ways.

It was the second evening of his coming.
Helen was playing dreamily, and humming
Some wordless melody of white-souled thought,
While Roy and I sat by the open door,
Re-living childish incidents of yore.
My eyes were glowing, and my cheeks were hot
With warm young blood, excitement, joy, or pain
Alike would send swift coursing through each vein.
Roy, always eloquent, was waxing fine,
And bringing vividly before my gaze
Some old adventure of those halcyon days,
When, suddenly, in pauses of the talk,
I heard a well-known step upon the walk,
And looked up quickly to meet full in mine
The eyes of Vivian Dangerfield. A flash
Shot from their depths :—a sudden blaze of light
Like that swift followed by the thunder's crash,
Which said, "Suspicion is confirmed by sight,"

As they fell on the pleasant doorway scene.
Then o'er his clear cut face, a cold white look
Crept, like the pallid moonlight o'er a brook,
And, with a slight, proud bending of the head,
He stepped toward us haughtily and said,
"Please pardon my intrusion, Miss Maurine:
I called to ask Miss Trevor for a book
She spoke of lending me: nay, sit you still!
And I, by grant of your permission, will
Pass by to where I hear her playing."
                                    "Stay!"
I said, "one moment, Vivian, if you please;"
And suddenly bereft of all my ease,
And scarcely knowing what to do, or say,
Confused as any school girl, I arose,
And some way made each to the other known.
They bowed, shook hands: then Vivian turned away,
And sought out Helen, leaving us alone.
(Men always shake hands—strangers, friends or foes,
While women only courtesy and bow,
Needing that space between them to allow
A fair inspection of each other's clothes.)

"One of Miss Trevor's, or of Maurine's beaux?
Which may he be, who cometh like a Prince
With haughty bearing, and an eagle eye?"
Roy queried, laughing: and I answered, "Since
You saw him pass me for Miss Trevor's side,
I leave your own good judgment to reply."

And straightway caused the tide of talk to glide
In other channels, striving to dispel
The sudden gloom that o'er my spirit fell.

We mortals are such hypocrites at best!
When Conscience tries our courage with a test,
And points to some steep pathway, we set out
Boldly, denying any fear or doubt;
But pause before the first rock in the way,
And, looking back, with tears, at Conscience, say,
"We are so sad dear Conscience! for we would
Most gladly do what to thee seemeth good;
But lo! this rock! we can not climb it, so
Thou must point out some other way to go."
Yet secretly we are rejoicing: and,
When right before our faces, as we stand
In seeming grief, the rock is cleft in twain,
Leaving the pathway clear, we shrink in pain!
And loth to go, by every act, reveal
What we so tried from Conscience to conceal.

I saw that hour, the way made plain, to do
With scarce an effort, what had seemed a strife
That would require the strength of my whole life.
Women have quick perceptions: and I knew
That Vivian's heart was full of jealous pain,
Suspecting—nay *believing* Roy Montaine

To be my lover. First my altered mien—
And next the letter—then the door-way scene—
My flushed face gazing in the one above
That bent so near me, and my strange confusion
When Vivian came, all led to one conclusion:
That I had but been playing with his love,
As women sometimes cruelly do play
With hearts what time their lovers are away.

There could be nothing easier, than just
To let him linger on in this belief
Till hourly-fed Suspicion and Distrust
Should turn to scorn and anger all his grief.
Compared with me, so doubly sweet and pure
Would Helen seem, my purpose would be sure,
And certain of completion in the end.
But now, the way was made so straight and clear,
My coward heart shrank back in guilty fear,
Till Conscience whispered with her "still small voice,"
" The precious time is passing—make thy choice—
Resign thy love, or slay thy trusting friend."

The growing moon, watched by the myriad eyes
Of countless stars, went sailing through the skies,
Like some young Prince, rising to rule a nation,
To whom all eyes are turned in expectation.

A woman who possesses tact and art
And strength of will can take the hand of doom,
And walk on, smiling sweetly as she goes,
With rosy lips, and rounded cheek of bloom,
Cheating a loud-tongued world that never knows
The pain and sorrow of her hidden heart.
And so I joined in Roy's bright changing chat;
Answered his sallies—talked of this and that,
My brow unruffled as the calm still wave
That tells not of the wrecked ship, and the grave
Beneath its surface.
    Then we heard, ere long,
The sound of Helen's gentle voice in song,
And, rising, entered where the subtle power
Of Vivian's eyes, forgiving while accusing,
Finding me weak, had won me, in that hour;
But Roy, alway polite and debonair
Where ladies were, now hung about my chair
With nameless delicate attentions, using
That air devotional, and those small arts
Acquaintance with society imparts
To men gallant by nature.
    'Twas my sex
And not myself he bowed to. Had my place
Been filled that evening by a dowager,
Twice his own age, he would have given her
The same attentions. But they served to vex
Whatever hope in Vivian's heart remained.
The cold, white look settled upon his face,
Telling how deeply he was hurt and pained.

Little by little, all things had conspired
To bring events I dreaded, yet desired.
We were in constant intercourse : walks, rides,
Picnics and sails, filled weeks of golden weather,
And almost hourly we were thrown together.
No words were spoken of rebuke or scorn :
Good friends we seemed. But as a gulf divides
This land and that—though lying side by side,
So rolled a gulf between us—deep and wide—
The gulf of doubt, which widened slowly morn
And noon and night.
     Free and informal were
These picnics and excursions. Yet, although
Helen and I would sometimes choose to go
Without our escorts, leaving them quite free,
It happened alway, Roy would seek out me
Ere passed the day, while Vivian walked with her.
I had no thought of flirting. Roy was just
Like some dear brother, and I quite forgot
The kinship was so distant it was not
Safe to rely upon in perfect trust,
Without reserve or caution. Many a time
When there was some steep mountain side to climb,
And I grew weary, he would say, " Maurine,
Come rest you here." And I would go and lean
My head upon his shoulder, or would stand
And let him hold in his my willing hand,
The while he stroked it gently with his own.
Or I would let him clasp me with his arm,
Nor entertained a thought of any harm !

Nor once supposed but Vivian was alone
In his suspicions. But ere long the truth
I learned in consternation ! both Aunt Ruth
And Helen, honestly, in faith believed
That Roy and I were lovers.
                              Undeceived,
Some careless words might open Vivian's eyes
And spoil my plans. So, reasoning in this wise,
To all their sallies I in jest replied,
To naught assented, and yet naught denied,
With Roy unchanged remaining, confident
Each understood just what the other meant.

If I grew weary of this double part,
And self-imposed deception caused my heart
Sometimes to shrink, I needed but to gaze
On Helen's face : that wore a look ethereal,
As if she dwelt above the things material
And held communion with the angels. So
I fed my strength and courage through the days.

What time the harvest moon rose full and clear
And cast its ling'ring radiance on the earth,
We made a feast ; and called, from far and near,
Our friends, who came to share the scene of mirth.
Fair forms and faces flitted to and fro ;
But none more sweet than Helen's. Robed in white,
She floated like a vision through the dance.

MAURINE.

So frailly fragile and so phantom fair,
She seemed like some stray spirit of the air,
And was pursued by many an anxious glance
That looked to see her fading from the sight
Like figures that a dreamer sees at night.

And noble men and gallants graced the scene:
Yet none more noble or more grand of mien
Than Vivian—broad of chest and shoulder, tall
And finely formed, as any Grecian god
Whose high-arched foot on Mount Olympus trod.
His clear cut face was beardless; and, like those
Same Grecian statues, when in calm repose,
Was it in hue and feature. Framed in hair
Dark and abundant; lighted by large eyes
That could be cold as steel in winter air,
Or warm and sunny as Italian skies.

Weary of mirth and music, and the sound
Of tripping feet, I sought a moment's rest
Within the lib'ry, where a group I found
Of guests, discussing with apparent zest
Some theme of interest—Vivian, near the while,
Leaning and listening with his slow odd smile.

"Now Miss La Pelle, we will appeal to you;"
Cried young Guy Semple, as I entered. "We

Have been discussing right before his face,
All unrebuked by him as you may see,
A poem lately published by our friend :
And we are quite divided. I contend
The poem is a libel and untrue.
I hold the fickle women are but few,
Compared with those who are like yon fair moon
That, ever faithful, rises in her place
Whether she's greeted by the flowers of June,
Or cold and dreary stretches of white space."

"O!" cried another, "Mr. Dangerfield
Look to your laurels! or you needs must yield
The crown to Semple, who, 'tis very plain,
Has mounted Pegasus and grasped his mane."

All laughed : and then, as Guy appealed to me,
I answered lightly, "My young friend, I fear
You chose a most unlucky simile
To prove the truth of woman. To her place
The moon does rise—but with a different face
Each time she comes. But now I needs must hear
The poem read, before I can consent
To pass my judgment on the sentiment."

All clamored that the author was the man
To read the poem : and, with tones that said

MAURINE.

More than the cutting, scornful words he read
Taking the book Guy gave him, he began:

HER LOVE.

    The sands upon the ocean side
    That change about with every tide,
    And never true to one abide,
        A woman's love I liken to.

    The summer zephyrs, light and vain,
    That sing the same alluring strain
    To every grass blade on the plain—
        A woman's love is nothing more.

    The sunshine of an April day
    That comes to warm you with its ray,
    But while you smile has flown away—
        A woman's love is like to this.

    God made poor woman with no heart,
    But gave her skill, and tact, and art,
    And so she lives, and plays her part.
        We must not blame, but pity her.

    She leans to man—but just to hear
    The praise he whispers in her ear.
    Herself, not him, she holdeth dear—
        O fool! to be deceived by her.

    To sate her selfish thirst she quaffs
    The love of strong hearts in sweet draughts,

> Then throws them lightly by and laughs,
>   Too weak to understand their pain.
>
>
> As changeful as the winds that blow
> From every region, to and fro,
> Devoid of heart, she can not know
>   The suffering of a human heart.

I knew the cold, fixed gaze of Vivian's eyes
Saw the slow color to my forehead rise;
But lightly answered, toying with my fan,
"That sentiment is very like a man!
Men call us fickle, but they do us wrong;
We're only frail and helpless, men are strong;
And when love dies, they take the poor dead thing
And make a shroud out of their suffering,
And carry the corpse about with them for years.
But we?—we mourn it for a day with tears!
And then we robe it for its last long rest,
But being women, feeble things at best,
We cannot dig the grave ourselves. And so
We call strong limbed New Love to lay it low:
Immortal sexton he! whom Venus sends
To do this service for her earthly friends.
The trusty fellow digs the grave so deep
Nothing disturbs the dead laid there to sleep."

The laugh that followed had not died away
Ere Roy Montaine came seeking me, to say

The band was tuning for our waltz, and so
Back to the ball room bore me. In the glow
And heat and whirl, my strength ere long was spent,
And I grew faint and dizzy, and we went
Into the cool moonlighted portico,
And, sitting there, Roy drew my languid head
Upon the shelter of his breast, and bent
His smiling eyes upon me, as he said,
"I'll try the mesmerism of my touch
To work a cure: be very quiet now,
And let me make some passes o'er your brow.
Why, how it throbs! you've exercised too much!
I shall not let you dance again to-night."

Just then before us, in the broad moonlight,
Two forms were mirrored: and I turned my face
To catch the teasing and mischievous glance
Of Helen's eyes, as, heated from the dance,
Leaning on Vivian's arm, she sought this place.

"I beg your pardon," came in that round tone
Of his low voice. "I think we do intrude."
Bowing, they turned, and left us quite alone
Ere I could speak, or change my attitude.

Part Fifth.

A visit to a cave some miles away
Was next in order. So, one sunny day,
Four prancing steeds conveyed a laughing load
Of merry pleasure-seekers o'er the road.
A basket picnic, music and croquet
Were in the programme. Skies were blue and clear,
And cool winds whispered of the Autumn near.
The merry-makers filled the time with pleasure;
Some floated to the music's rhythmic measure,
Some played, some promenaded on the green.

Ticked off by happy hearts, the moments passed.
The afternoon, all glow and glimmer, came.
Helen and Roy were leaders of some game,
And Vivian was not visible.
                    "Maurine,
I challenge you to climb yon cliff with me!
And who shall tire, or reach the summit last
Must pay a forfeit," cried a romping maid.
"Come! start at once, or own you are afraid."

So challenged I made ready for the race,
Deciding first the forfeit was to be
A handsome pair of bootees to replace
The victor's loss who made the rough ascent.
The cliff was steep and stony. On we went
As eagerly as if the path was Fame,
And what we climbed for, glory and a name.

My hands were bruised; my garments sadly rent,
But on I clambered. Soon I heard a cry,
"Maurine! Maurine! my strength is wholly spent!
You've won the boots! I'm going back—good-by!"
And back she turned, in spite of laugh and jeer.
I reached the summit: and its solitude,
Wherein no living creature did intrude,
Save some sad birds that wheeled and circled near,
I found far sweeter than the scene below.
Alone with One who knew my hidden woe,
I did not feel so much alone as when
I mixed with th' unthinking throngs of men.

Some flowers that decked the barren, sterile place
I plucked, and read the lesson they conveyed,
That in our lives, albeit dark with shade
And rough and hard with labor, yet may grow
The flowers of Patience, Sympathy, and Grace.

As I walked on in meditative thought,
A serpent writhed across my pathway—not
A large or deadly serpent; yet the sight
Filled me with ghastly terror and affright.
I shrieked aloud: a darkness veiled my eyes—
And I fell fainting 'neath the watchful skies.

I was no coward. Country-bred and born,
I had no feeling but the keenest scorn
For those fine lady "ah's" and "oh's" of fear
So much assumed, (when any man is near.)
But God implanted in each human heart
A natural horror, and a sickly dread
Of that accurs-ed, slimy, creeping thing
That squirms a limbless carcass o'er the ground.
And where that inborn loathing is not found
You'll find the serpent-qualities instead.
Who fears it not, himself is next of kin,
And in his bosom holds some treacherous art
Whereby to counteract its venomed sting.
And all are sired by Satan—Chief of Sin.

Who loathes not that foul creature of the dust,
However fair in seeming, I distrust.

I woke from my unconsciousness, to know
I leaned upon a broad and manly breast,

And Vivian's voice was speaking soft and low,
Sweet whispered words of passion, o'er and o'er.
I dared not breathe. Had I found Eden's shore?
Was this a foretaste of eternal bliss?
"My love," he sighed, his voice like winds that moan
Before a rain in summer time, "My own,
For one sweet stolen moment, lie and rest
Upon this heart that loves and hates you both!
O fair false face! Why were you made so fair!
O mouth of Southern sweetness! that ripe kiss
That hangs upon you, I do take an oath
His lips shall never gather. There!—and there!
I steal it from him. Are you his—all his?
Nay you are mine, this moment, as I dreamed—
Blind fool—believing you were what you seemed—
You would be mine in all the years to come.
Fair fiend! I love and hate you in a breath.
O God! if this white pallor were but *death*,
And I were stretched beside you, cold and dumb,
My arms about you, so—in fond embrace!
My lips pressed, so—upon your dying face!"

"Woman, how dare you bring me to such shame!
How dare you drive me to an act like this,
To steal from your unconscious lips the kiss
You lured me on to think my rightful claim!
O frail and puny woman! could you know
The devil that you waken in the hearts
You snare and bind in your enticing arts,

The thin, pale stuff that in your veins doth flow
Would freeze in terror.
                    Strange you have such pow'r
To please, or pain us, poor, weak, soulless things—
Devoid of passion as a senseless flow'r!
Like butterflies, your only boast, your wings.
There, now, I scorn you—scorn you from this hour,
And hate myself for having talked of love!"

He pushed me from him. And I felt as those
Doomed angels must, when pearly gates above
Are closed against them.
                    With a feigned surprise
I started up, and opened wide my eyes,
And looked about. Then in confusion rose
And stood before him.
                    "Pardon me, I pray!"
He said quite coldly. "Half an hour ago
I left you with the company below,
And sought this cliff. A moment since you cried,
It seemed, in sudden terror and alarm.
I came in time to see you swoon away.
You'll need assistance down the rugged side
Of this steep cliff. I pray you take my arm."

So, formal and constrained, we passed along,
Rejoined our friends, and mingled with the throng,
To have no further speech again that day.

Next morn there came a bulky document,
The legal firm of Blank & Blank had sent,
Containing news unlooked for. An estate
Which proved a cosy fortune--no-wise great
Or princely,--had in France been left to me,
My grandsire's last descendant. And it brought
A sense of joy and freedom in the thought
Of foreign travel, which I felt would be
A panacea for my troubled mind,
That longed to leave the olden scenes behind
With all their recollections, and to flee
To some strange country.
      I was in such haste
To put between me and my native land
The briny ocean's desolating waste,
I gave Aunt Ruth no peace, until she planned
To sail that week, two months : though she was fain
To wait until the Spring time. Roy Montaine
Would be our guide and escort.
       No one dreamed
The cause of my strange hurry, but all seemed
To think good fortune had quite turned my brain.
One bright October morning, when the woods
Had donned their purple mantles and red hoods
In honor of the Frost King, Vivian came,
Bringing some green leaves, tipped with crimsom
   flame,—
First trophies of the autumn time.
        And Roy
Made a proposal that we all should go

And ramble in the forest for a while.
But Helen said she was not well—and so
Must stay at home. Then Vivian with a smile
Responded, "I will stay and talk to you,
And they may go;" at which her two cheeks grew
Like twin blush roses;—dyed with love's red wave,
Her fair face shone transfigured with great joy.

And Vivian saw—and suddenly was grave.

Roy took my arm in that protecting way
Peculiar to some men, which seems to say
"I shield my own," a manner pleasing, e'en
When we are conscious that it does not mean
More than a simple courtesy. A woman
Whose heart is wholly feminine and human,
And not unsexed by hobbies, likes to be
The object of that tender chivalry,—
That guardianship which man bestows on her,
Yet mixed with deference; as if she were
Half child, half angel.
              Though she may be strong,
Noble and self-reliant, not afraid
To raise her voice and hand against all wrong
And all oppression, yet if she be made,
With all the independence of her thought,
A woman womanly, as God designed,
Albeit she may have as great a mind

As man, her brother, yet his strength of arm,
His muscle and his boldness she has not,
And cannot have, without she loses what
Is far more precious, modesty and grace.
So, walking on, in her appointed place,
She does not strive to ape him, nor pretend
But that she needs him, for a guide and friend,
To shield her with his greater strength from harm.

We reached the forest; wandered to and fro
Through many a winding path and dim retreat,
Till I grew weary: when I chose a seat
Upon an oak tree, which had been laid low
By some wind storm, or by some lightning stroke.
And Roy stood just below me, where the ledge
On which I sat sloped steeply to the edge
Of sunny meadows lying at my feet.
One hand held mine; the other grasped a limb
That cast its checkered shadows over him;
And, with his head thrown back, his dark eyes raised
And fixed upon me, silently he gazed
Until I, smiling, turned to him and spoke:
"Give words, my cousin, to those thoughts that rise,
And, like dumb spirits, look forth from your eyes."

The smooth and even darkness of his cheek
Was stained one moment by a flush of red.
He swayed his lithe form nearer as he stood

Still clinging to the branch above his head.
His brilliant eyes grew darker; and he said,
With sudden passion, "Do you bid me speak?
I can not, then, keep silence if I would.
That hateful fortune, coming as it did,
Forbade my speaking sooner; for I knew
A harsh-tongued world would quickly misconstrue
My motive for a meaner one. But, sweet,
So big my heart has grown with love for you
I can not shelter it, or keep it hid.
And so I cast it throbbing at your feet,
For you to guard and cherish, or to break.
Maurine, I love you better than my life.
My friend—my cousin—be still more, my wife!
Maurine, Maurine, what answer do you make?"

I scarce could breathe for wonderment; and numb
With truth that fell too suddenly, sat dumb
With sheer amaze, and stared at Roy with eyes
That looked no feeling but complete surprise.
He swayed so near his breath was on my cheek.
"Maurine, Maurine," he whispered, "will you speak?"

Then suddenly, as o'er some magic glass
One picture in a score of shapes will pass,
I seemed to see Roy glide before my gaze.
First, as the playmate of my earlier days—
Next, as my kin—and then my valued friend,

MAURINE.

And last, my lover. As when colors blend
In some unlooked for group before our eyes,
We hold the glass, and look them o'er and o'er,
So now I gazed on Roy in his new guise,
In which he ne'er appeared to me before.

His form was like a panther's in its grace,
So lithe and supple, and of medium height,
And garbed in all the elegance of fashion.
His large black eyes were full of fire and passion,
And in expression fearless, firm, and bright.
His hair was like the very deeps of night,
And hung in raven clusters 'round a face
Of dark and flashing beauty.
      He was more
Like some romantic maiden's grand ideal
Than like a common being. As I gazed
Upon the handsome face to mine upraised,
I saw before me, living, breathing, real
The hero of my early day-dreams: though
So full my heart was with that clear-cut face,
Which, all unlike, yet claimed the hero's place,
I had not recognized him so before,
Or thought of him, save as a valued friend.
So now I called him, adding,
       "Foolish boy!
Each word of love you utter aims a blow
At that sweet trust I had reposed in you.
I was so certain I had found a true,

Steadfast man friend, on whom I could depend,
And go on wholly trusting, to the end.
Why did you shatter my delusion, Roy,
By turning to a lover?"
      "Why, indeed!
Because I loved you more than any brother,
Or any friend could love." Then he began
To argue like a lawyer, and to plead
With all his eloquence. And, listening,
I strove to think it was a goodly thing
To be so fondly loved by such a man,
And it were best to give his wooing heed,
And not deny him. Then before my eyes
In all its clear-cut majesty, that other
Haughty and poet-handsome face would rise
And rob my purpose of all life and strength.

Roy urged and argued, as Roy only could,
With that impetuous, boyish eloquence.
He held my hands, and vowed I must, and should
Give some least hope; till, in my own defense,
I turned upon him, and replied, at length:
"I thank you for the noble heart you offer:
But it deserves a true one in exchange.
I could love you if I loved not another
Who keeps my heart; so I have none to proffer."

Then, seeing how his dark eyes flashed, I said,
"Dear Roy! I know my words seem very strange;

MAURINE.

But I love one I cannot hope to wed.
A river rolls between us, dark and deep.
To cross it—were to stain with blood my hand.
You force my speech on what I fain would keep
In my own bosom, but you understand?
My heart is given to love that's sanctified,
And now can feel no other.
      Be you kind
Dear Roy, my brother! speak of this no more,
Lest pleading and denying should divide
The hearts so long united. Let me find
In you my cousin and my friend of yore.
And now come home. The morning, all too soon
And unperceived, has melted into noon.
Helen will miss us, and we must return."

He took my hand, and helped me to arise,
Smiling upon me with his sad dark eyes,
Wherein no fire of passion now did burn.

"And so," he said, "too soon and unforeseen
My friendship melted into love, Maurine.
But, sweet! I am not wholly in the blame,
For what you term my folly. You forgot,
So long we'd known each other, I had not
In truth a brother or a cousin's claim.
But I remembered, when through every nerve
Your lightest touch went thrilling; and began

To love you with that human love of man
For comely woman. By your coaxing arts,
You won your way into my heart of hearts,
And all Platonic feelings put to rout.
A maid should never lay aside reserve
With one who's not her kinsman, out and out.
But as we now, with measured steps, retrace
The path we came, e'en so my heart I'll send,
At your command, back to the olden place,
And strive to love you only as a friend."
I felt the justice of his mild reproof,
But answered laughing, "'Tis the same old cry:
'The woman tempted me, and I did eat.'
Since Adam's time we've heard it. But I'll try
And be more prudent, sir, and hold aloof
The fruit I never once had thought so sweet
'Twould tempt you any. Now go dress for dinner,
Thou sinned against! as also will the sinner.
And guard each act, that no least look betray
What's passed between us."
     Then I turned away
And sought my room, trilling some lightsome air
That ceased upon the threshold; for mine eyes
Fell on a face so glorified and fair
All other senses, merged in that of sight,
Were lost in contemplation of the bright
And wond'rous picture, which had otherwise
Made dim my vision.
    Waiting in my room,
Her whole face lit as by an inward flame

That shed its halo 'round her, Helen stood ;
Her fair hands folded like a lily's leaves
Weighed down by happy dews of summer eves.
Upon her cheek the color went and came
As sunlight flickers o'er a bed of bloom :
And, like some slim young sapling of the wood,
Her slender form leaned slightly ; and her hair
Fell 'round her loosely, in long curling strands
All unconfined, and as by loving hands
Tossed into bright confusion.
      Standing there,
Her starry eyes uplifted, she did seem
Like some unearthly creature of a dream ;
Until she started forward, gliding slowly,
And broke the breathless silence, speaking lowly,
As one grown meek, and humble in an hour,
Bowing before some new and mighty power.

"Maurine, Maurine!" she murmured, and again,
"Maurine, my own sweet friend, Maurine!"
        And then,
Laying her love light hands upon my head,
She leaned, and looked into my eyes, and said
With voice that bore her joy in ev'ry tone,
As winds that blow across a garden bed
Are weighed with fragrance, "He is mine alone,
And I am his—all his—his very own.
So pledged this hour, by that most sacred tie
Save one beneath God's over-arching sky.

I could not wait to tell you of my bliss:
I want your blessing, sweetheart! and your kiss."
So hiding my heart's trouble with a smile,
I leaned and kissed her dainty mouth; the while
I felt a guilt-joy, as of some sweet sin,
When my lips fell where his so late had been.
And all day long I bore about with me
A sense of shame—yet mixed with satisfaction,
As some starved child might steal a loaf, and be
Sad with the guilt resulting from her action,
While yet the morsel in her mouth was sweet.
That ev'ning when the house had settled down
To sleep and quiet, to my room there crept
A lithe young form, robed in a long white gown:
With steps like fall of thistle-down she came,
Her mouth smile-wreathed; and, breathing low my name,
Nestled in graceful beauty at my feet.

"Sweetheart," she murmured softly, "ere I slept,
I needs must tell you all my tale of joy.
Beginning where you left us—you and Roy.
You saw the color flame upon my cheek
When Vivian spoke of staying. So did he;—
And, when we were alone, he gazed at me
With such a strange look in his wondrous eyes.
The silence deepened; and I tried to speak
Upon some common topic, but could not,
My heart was in such tumult.

"In this wise
Five happy moments glided by us, fraught
With hours of feeling. Vivian rose up then,
And came and stood by me, and stroked my hair,
And, in his low voice, o'er and o'er again,
Said 'Helen, little Helen, frail and fair.'
Then took my face, and turned it to the light,
And looking in my eyes, and seeing what,
Was shining from them, murmured, sweet and low,
'Dear eyes, you cannot veil the truth from sight.
You love me Helen! answer, is it so?'
And I made answer straightway, 'With my life
And soul, and strength I love you, O my love!'
He leaned and took me gently to his breast,
And said, 'Here then, this dainty head shall rest
Henceforth forever: O my little dove!
My lily-bud—my fragile blossom-wife!'"

"And then I told him all my thoughts; and he
Listened, with kisses for his comments, till
My tale was finished. Then he said, 'I will
Be frank with you my darling from the start,
And hide no secret from you in my heart.
I love you Helen, but you are not first
To rouse that love to being. Ere we met
I loved a woman madly—never dreaming
She was not all in truth she was in seeming.
Enough! she proved to be that thing accursed
Of God and man—a wily vain coquette.

I hate myself for having loved her. Yet
So much my heart spent on her, it must give
A love less ardent, and less prodigal,
Albeit just as tender and as true—
A milder, yet a faithful love to you.
Just as some evil fortune might befall
A man's great riches, causing him to live
In some low cot, all unpretending, still
As much his home—as much his loved retreat,
As was the princely palace on the hill,
E'en so I give you all that's left, my sweet !
Of my heart-fortune."

      " 'That were more to me,'
I made swift smiling answer, 'than to be
The worshipped consort of a King.' And so
Our faith was pledged. But Vivian would not go
Until I vowed to wed him New Year day.
And I am sad because you go away
Before that time. I shall not feel half wed
Without you here. Postpone your trip and stay,
And be my bridesmaid."

      " Nay, I cannot, dear !
'Twould disarrange our plans for half a year.
I'll be in Europe New Year day," I said,
" And send congratulations by the cable."
And from my soul thanked Providence for sparing
The pain, to me, of sharing in, and wearing
The festal garments of a wedding scene,
While all my heart was hung with sorrow's sable.

Forgetting for a season, that between
The cup and lip lies many a chance of loss,
I lived in my near future, confident
All would be as I planned it; and, across
The briny waste of waters, I should find
Some balm and comfort for my troubled mind.
The sad fall days, like maidens auburn-tressed
And amber-eyed, in purple garments dressed,
Passed by, and dropped their tears upon the tomb
Of fair Queen Summer, buried in her bloom.
Roy left us for a time, and Helen went
To make the nuptial preparations. Then,
Aunt Ruth complained one day of feeling ill:
Her veins ran red with fever; and the skill
Of two physicians could not stem the tide.
The house, that rang so late with laugh and jest,
Grew ghostly with low whispered sounds: and when
The Autumn day that I had thought to be
Bounding upon the billows of the sea
Came sobbing in, it found me pale and worn,
Striving to keep away that unloved guest
Who comes unbidden, making hearts to mourn.

Through all the anxious weeks I watched beside
The suff'rer's couch, Roy was my help and stay;
Others were kind, but he alone each day,
Brought strength and comfort by his cheerful face
And hopeful words, that fell in that sad place
Like rays of light upon a darkened way.

November passed; and winter, crisp and chill,
In robes of ermine walked on plain and hill.
Returning light and life dispelled the gloom
That cheated Death had brought us from the tomb.
Aunt Ruth was saved, and slowly getting better—
Was dressed each day, and walked about the room.
Then came one morning in the Eastern mail,
A little white winged birdling of a letter.
I broke the seal, and read,
                              "Maurine, my own!
I hear Aunt Ruth is better, and am glad.
I felt so sorry for you; and so sad
To think I left you when I did—alone
To bear your pain and worry, and those nights
Of weary anxious watching.
                              "Vivian writes
Your plans are changed now, and you will not sail
Before the Spring time. So you'll come and be
My bridesmaid, darling! Do not say me nay.
But three weeks more of girlhood left to me.
Come, if you can, just two weeks from to-day,
And make your preparations here. My sweet!
Indeed I am not glad Aunt Ruth was ill—
I'm sorry she has suffered so; and still
I'm thankful something happened, so you stayed.
I'm sure my wedding would be incomplete
Without your presence. Selfish, I'm afraid
You'll think your Helen. But I love you so,
How can I be quite willing you should go?
Come Christmas Eve, or earlier. Let me know

MAURINE.

And I will meet you, dearie! at the train.
Your happy loving Helen."
                              Then the pain
That, hidden under later pain and care,
Had made no moan, but silent, seemed to sleep,
Woke from its trance-like lethargy, to steep
My tortured heart in anguish and despair.

I had relied too fully on my skill
In bending circumstances to my will:
And now I was rebuked, and made to see
That God alone knoweth what is to be.
Then came a messenger from Vivian, who
Came not himself as he was wont to do,
But sent his servant each new day to bring
A kindly message, or an offering
Of juicy fruits, to cool the lips of fever,
Or dainty hot-house blossoms, with their bloom
To brighten up the convalescent's room.
But now the servant only brought a line
From Vivian Dangerfield to Roy Montaine.
"Dear Sir, and Friend"—in letters bold and plain,
Written on cream-white paper, so it ran:
"It is the will and pleasure of Miss Trevor,
And therefore doubly so a wish of mine,
That you shall honor me next New Year Eve,
My wedding hour, by standing as best man.
Miss Trevor has six bridesmaids I believe.
Being myself a novice in the art—

If I should fail in acting well my part,
I'll need protection 'gainst the regiment
Of outraged females. So I pray, consent
To stand by me in time of need, and shield
Your friend sincerely, Vivian Dangerfield."

The last least hope has vanished; I must drain,
E'en to the dregs, this bitter cup of pain.

Part Sixth.

There was a week of bustle and of hurry;
A stately home echoed to voices sweet,
Calling, replying; and to tripping feet
Of busy bridesmaids, running to and fro,
With all that girlish fluttering and flurry
Preceding such occasions. Helen's room
Was like a lily-garden, all in bloom,
Decked with the dainty robes of her trousseau.
  My robe was fashioned by swift, skillful hands—
A thing of beauty, elegant and rich,
A mystery of loopings, puffs and bands;
And as I watched it growing, stitch by stitch,
I felt as one might feel who did behold
With vision trance-like, where his body lay
In deathly slumber, simulating clay,
His grave-cloth sewed together, fold on fold.

I lived with ev'ry nerve upon the strain,
As men go into battle; and the pain,
That, more and more, to my sad heart revealed,
Grew ghastly with its horrors, was concealed

From mortal eyes by superhuman pow'r,
That God bestowed upon me, hour by hour.

    What night the Old Year gave unto the New
The key of human happiness and woe,
The pointed stars, upon their field of blue,
Shone, white and perfect, o'er a world below,
Of snow-clad beauty; all the trees were dressed
In gleaming garments, decked with diadems,
Each seeming like a bridal-bidden guest,
Coming o'er-laden with a gift of gems.

The bustle of the dressing-room; the sound
Of eager voices in discourse; the clang
Of "sweet bells jangled"; thud of steel-clad feet
That beat swift music on the frozen ground—
All blent together in my brain, and rang
A medley of strange noises, incomplete,
And full of discords.   Then out on the night
Streamed, from the open vestibule, a light
That lit the velvet blossoms which we trod,
With all the hues of those that deck the sod.
The grand cathedral windows were ablaze
With gorgeous colors: through a sea of bloom,
Up the long aisle, to join the waiting groom,
The bridal cortege passed.

MAURINE.

                        As some lost soul
Might surge on with the curious crowd, to gaze
Upon its coffined body, so I went
With that glad festal throng. The organ sent
Great waves of melody along the air,
That broke and fell, in liquid drops, like spray,
On happy hearts that listened. But to me
It sounded faintly, as if miles away
A troubled spirit, sitting in despair
Beside the sad and ever-moaning sea,
Gave utterance to sighing sounds of dole.

We paused before the altar. Framed in flowers,
The white-robed man of God stood forth.
                                        I heard
The solemn service open; through long hours
I seemed to stand and listen, while each word
Fell on my ear as falls the sound of clay
Upon the coffin of the worshipped dead.
The stately father gave the bride away:
The bridegroom circled with a golden band
The taper finger of her dainty hand.
The last imposing, binding words were said—
"What God has joined let no man put asunder"
And all my strife with self was at an end;
My lover was the husband of my friend.

How strangely, in some awful hour of pain,
External trifles with our sorrows blend!

I never hear the mighty organ's thunder,
I never catch the scent of heliotrope,
Nor see stained windows all ablaze with light,
Without that dizzy whirling of the brain,
And all the ghastly feelings of that night,
When my sick heart relinquished love and hope.

The pain we felt so keenly may depart,
And e'en its memory cease to haunt the heart;
But some slight thing, a perfume, or a sound
Will probe the closed recesses of the wound,
And for a moment bring the old-time smart.

Congratulations, kisses, tears and smiles,
Good-byes and farewells given; then across
The snowy waste of weary wintry miles,
Back to my girlhood's home, where, through each
      room,
Forever more pale phantoms of delight
Should aimless wander, alway in my sight,
Pointing, with ghostly fingers, to the tomb
Wet with the tears of living pain and loss.

The sleepless nights of watching and of care,
Followed by that one week of keenest pain,
Taxing my weakened system, and my brain,
Brought on a ling'ring illness.

                                        Day by day,
In that strange, apathetic state I lay,
Of mental and of physical despair.
I had no pain, no fever, and no chill,
But lay without ambition, strength, or will,
Knowing no wish for anything but rest,
Which seemed, of all God's store of gifts, the best.

Physicians came and shook their heads and sighed:
And to their score of questions I replied,
With but one languid answer, o'er and o'er,
" I am so weary—weary—nothing more."

I slept, and dreamed I was some feathered thing,
Flying through space with ever-aching wing,
Seeking a ship called Rest, all snowy white,
That sailed and sailed before me, just in sight,
But alway one unchanging distance kept,
And woke more weary than before I slept.

I slept, and dreamed I ran to win a prize,
A hand from Heaven held down before my eyes.
All eagerness, I sought it—it was gone;
But shone in all its beauty farther on.
I ran, and ran, and ran, in eager quest
Of that great prize, whereon was written "rest."

Which ever just beyond my reach did gleam,
And wakened doubly weary with my dream.

I dreamed I was a crystal drop of rain,
That saw a snow-white lily on the plain,
And left the cloud to nestle in her breast.
I fell and fell, but never more found rest—
I fell and fell, but found no stopping place,
Through leagues and leagues of never-ending space,
While space illimitable stretched before.

And all these dreams but wearied me the more.

Familiar voices sounded in my room—
Aunt Ruth's, and Roy's, and Helen's: but they
            seemed
A part of some strange fancy I had dreamed,
And now remembered dimly.
                        Wrapped in gloom,
My mind, o'er-taxed, lost hold of time at last,
Ignored its future, and forgot its past,
And groped along the present, as a light,
Carried, uncovered, through the fogs of night,
Will flicker faintly.
                    But I felt, at length,
When March winds brought vague rumors of the
          Spring,

A certain sense of "restlessness with rest."
My aching frame was weary of repose,
And wanted action.
                    Then slow-creeping strength
Came back with Mem'ry, hand in hand, to bring
And lay upon my sore and bleeding breast,
Grim-visaged Recollection's thorny rose.
   I gained, and failed. One day could ride and
        walk,
The next would find me prostrate: while a flock
Of ghostly thoughts, like phantom birds, would flit
About the chambers of my heart, or sit,
Pale spectres of the past, with folded wings,
Perched, silently, upon the voiceless strings,
That once resounded to Hope's happy lays.

So passed the ever-changing April days.
When May came, lightsome footed, o'er the lea,
Accompanied by kind Aunt Ruth and Roy,
I bade farewell to home with secret joy,
And turned my wan face eastward, to the sea.
Roy planned our route of travel: for all lands
Were one to him. Or Egypt's burning sands,
Or Alps of Switzerland, or stately Rome,
All were familiar as the fields of home.

There was a year of wand'ring to and fro,
Like restless spirits; scaling mountain heights;

Dwelling among the countless, rare delights
Of lands historic; turning dusty pages,
Stamped with the tragedies of mighty ages;
Gazing upon the scenes of bloody acts,
Of kings long buried—bare, unvarnished facts,
Surpassing wildest fictions of the brain;
Rubbing against all people, high and low,
And by this contact feeling Self to grow
Smaller and less important, and the vein
Of human kindness deeper, seeing God,
Unto the humble delver on the sod,
And to the ruling monarch on the throne,
Has given hope, ambition, joy, and pain,
And that all hearts have feelings like our own.

●

There is no school that disciplines the mind,
And broadens thought, like contact with mankind.
The college-prisoned greybeard, who has burned
The midnight lamp, and book-bound knowledge
    learned,
Till sciences or classics hold no lore
He has not conned and studied, o'er and o'er,
Is but a babe in wisdom, when compared
With some unlettered wand'rer, who has shared
The hospitalities of every land;
Felt touch of brother in each proffered hand;
Made man his study, and the world his college,
And gained this grand epitome of knowledge:

Each human being has a heart and soul,
And self is but an atom of the whole.

I hold he is best learn-ed, and most wise,
Who best and most can love and sympathize.
Book-wisdom makes us vain and self-contained;
Our banded minds go 'round in little grooves;
But constant friction with the world removes
These iron foes to freedom, and we rise
To grander heights, and, all untrammeled, find
A better atmosphere and clearer skies;
And through its broadened realm, no longer chained,
Thought-travels freely, leaving Self behind.

Where'er we chanced to wander, or to roam,
Glad letters came from Helen; happy things
Like little birds that followed on swift wings,
Bringing their tender messages from home.
"Her days were poems, beautiful complete.
The rhythm perfect, and the burden sweet.
She was so happy—happy, and so blest."

My heart had found contentment in that year.
With health restored, my life seemed full of cheer.
The heart of youth turns ever to the light;
Sorrow and gloom may curtain it like night,
But, in its very anguish and unrest,

It beats and tears the pall-like folds away,
And finds again the sunlight of the day.

And yet, despite the changes without measure,
Despite sight-seeing, round on round of pleasure ;
Despite new friends, new suitors, still my heart
Was conscious of a something lacking, where
Love once had dwelt, and afterward despair.
Now love was buried ; and despair had flown
Before the healthful zephyrs that had blown
From heights serene and lofty ; and the place
Where both had dwelt, was empty voiceless space.
And so I took my long loved study, art,
The dreary longing in my life to fill,
And worked, and labored, with a right good will.
Aunt Ruth and I took rooms in Rome ; while Roy
Lingered in Scotland, with his new found joy.
A dainty little lassie, Grace Kildare
Had snared him in her flossy, flaxen hair,
And made him captive.
     We were thrown, by chance,
In contact with her people while in France
The previous season : she was wholly sweet
And fair and gentle ; so naive, and yet
So womanly, she was at once the pet
Of all our party ; and, ere many days,
Won by her fresh face, and her artless ways,
Roy fell a helpless captive at her feet.
Her home was in the Highlands ; and she came

Of good old stock, of fair untarnished fame.
Through all these months Roy had been true as steel ;
And by his every action made me feel
He was my friend and brother, and no more.
The same big-souled and trusty friend of yore.
Yet, in my secret heart, I wished I knew,
Whether the love he felt one time was dead,
Or only hidden, for my sake, from view.
So when he came to me one day, and said,
The velvet blackness of his eyes ashine
With light of love and triumph: "Cousin, mine!
Congratulate me! She whom I adore
Has pledged to me the promise of her hand ;
Her heart I have already." I was glad
With double gladness, for it freed my mind
From fear that he, in secret, might be sad.

From March till June had left her moons behind,
And merged her rose-red beauty in July,
There was no message from my native land.
Then came a few brief lines, by Vivian penned :
"Death had been near to Helen, but passed by ;
The danger was now over. God was kind ;
The mother and the child were both alive ;
No other child was ever known to thrive
As throve this one, nurse had been heard to say.
The infant was a wonder, every way.
And, at command of Helen, he would send,
A lock of baby's golden hair to me.

And did I, on my honor, ever see
Such hair before? Helen would write, ere long :
She gained quite slowly, but would soon be strong—
Stronger than ever, so the doctors said."

I took the tiny ringlet, golden—fair,
Mayhap his hand had severed from the head
Of his own child, and pressed it to my cheek
And to my lips, and kissed it o'er and o'er.
All my maternal instincts seemed to rise,
And clamor for their rights, while my wet eyes,
Rained tears upon the silken tress of hair.
The woman struggled with her heart before!
It was, the mother in me now did speak,
Moaning, like Rachel, that her babes were not,
And crying out against her barren lot.

Once I bemoaned the long and lonely years
That stretched before me, dark with love's eclipse ;
And thought how my unmated heart would miss
The shelter of a broad and manly breast—
The strong, bold arm—the tender clinging kiss—
And all pure love's possessions, manifold ;
But now I wept a flood of bitter tears,
Thinking of little heads of shining gold,
That would not on my bosom sink to rest ;
Of little hands that would not touch my cheek ;
Of little lisping voices, and sweet lips,

That never in my list'ning ear would speak
The blessed name of mother.
                        O, in woman
How mighty is the love of offspring! Ere
Unto her wond'ring, untaught mind unfolds
The myst'ry that is half divine, half human,
Of life and birth, the love of unborn souls
Within her, and the mother-yearning creeps
Through her warm heart, and stirs its hidden deeps,
And grows and strengthens with each riper year.

As storms may gather in a placid sky,
And spend their fury, and then pass away,
Leaving again the blue of cloudless day,
E'en so the tempest of my grief passed by.
'Twas weak to mourn for what I had resigned,
With the deliberate purpose of my mind,
To my sweet friend.
                    Relinquishing my love,
I gave my dearest hope of joy to her.
If God, from out his boundless store above,
Had chosen added blessings to confer,
I would rejoice, for her sake—not repine,
That th' immortal treasures were not mine.

Better my lonely sorrow, than to know
My selfish joy had been another's woe;
Better my grief and my strength to control,

Than the despair of her frail-bodied soul;
Better to go on, loveless, to the end,
Than wear love's rose, whose thorn had slain friend.

Work is the salve that heals the wounded heart.
With will most resolute I set my aim
To enter on the weary race for Fame,
And if I failed to climb the dizzy height,
To reach some point of excellence in art.

E'en as the Maker held earth incomplete,
Till man was formed, and placed upon the sod,
The perfect, living image of his God,
All landscape scenes were lacking in my sight,
Wherein the human figure had no part.
In that, all lines of symmetry did meet—
All hues of beauty mingle. So I brought
Enthusiasm in abundance, thought,
Much study, and some talent, day by day,
To help me in my efforts to portray
The wondrous power, majesty and grace
Stamped on some form, or looking from some face
This was to be my specialty: To take
Human emotion for my theme, and make
The unassisted form divine express,
Anger or Sorrow, Pleasure, Pain, Distress;

And thus to build Fame's monument above
The grave of my departed hope and love.

This is not Genius. Genius spreads its wings
And soars beyond itself, or selfish things.
Talent has need of stepping stones: some cross,
Some cheated purpose, some great pain or loss,
Must lay the groundwork, and arouse ambition,
Before it labors onward to fruition.

But, as the lark from beds of bloom will rise
And sail and sing among the very skies,
Still mounting near and nearer to the light,
Impelled alone by love of upward flight,
So Genius soars—it does not need to climb—
Upon God-given wings, to heights sublime.
Some sportsman's shot, grazing the singer's throat,
Some venomous assault of birds of prey,
May speed its flight toward the realm of day,
And tinge with triumph every liquid note.
So deathless Genius mounts but higher yet,
When Strife and Envy think to slay or fret.

There is no balking Genius. Only death
Can silence it—or hinder. While there's breath
Or sense of feeling, it will spurn the sod,
And lift itself to glory, and to God.

The acorn sprouted—weeds nor flowers can choke
The certain growth of th' upreaching oak.

Talent was mine, not Genius; and my mind
Seemed bound by chains, and would not leave behind
Its selfish love and sorrow.
                            Did I strive
To picture some emotion, lo! *his* eyes,
Of emerald beauty, dark as ocean dyes,
Looked from the canvas: and my buried pain
Rose from its grave, and stood by me alive.
Whate'er my subject, in some hue or line,
The glorious beauty of his face would shine.

So, for a time, my labor seemed in vain,
Since it but freshened, and made keener yet,
The grief my heart was striving to forget.

While in his form all strength and magnitude
With grace and supple sinews were entwined,
While in his face all beauties were combined
Of perfect features, intellect and truth,
With all that fine rich coloring of youth,
How could my brush portray aught good or fair
Wherein no fatal likeness did intrude
Of him my soul had worshipped?

MAURINE.

                        But, at last,
Setting a watch upon my unwise heart
That thus would mix its sorrow with my art,
I resolutely shut away the past,
And made the toilsome present passing bright
With dreams of what was hidden from my sight
In the far distant future, when the soil
Should yield me golden fruit for all my toil.

PART SEVENTH.

With much hard labor and some pleasure fraught,
The months rolled by me noiselessly, that taught
My hand to grow more skillful in its art,
Strengthened my daring dream of fame, and brought
Sweet hope and resignation to my heart.

Brief letters came from Helen, now and then:
"She was quite well—oh, yes! quite well, indeed!
But still so weak and nervous. By and by,
When baby, being older, should not need
Such constant care, she would grow strong again.
She was as happy as a soul could be;
No least cloud hovered in her azure sky;
She had not thought life had such depths of bliss.
Dear baby sent Maurine a loving kiss,
And said she was a naughty, naughty girl,
Not to come home and see ma's little pearl."

No gift of costly jewels, or of gold,
Had been so precious or so dear to me,
As each brief line wherein her joy was told.

It lightened toil, and took the edge from pain,
Knowing my sacrifice was not in vain.

Roy purchased fine estates in Scotland, where
He built a pretty villa-like retreat.
And when the Roman summer's languid heat
Made work a punishment, I turned my face
Toward the Highlands, and with Roy and Grace
Found rest and freedom from all thought and care.

I was a willing worker. Not an hour
Passed idly by me : each, I did employ
To some good purpose, ere it glided on
To swell the tide of hours forever gone.
My first completed picture, known as " Joy "
Won pleasant words of praise. " Possesses pow'r,"
" Displays much talent," " Very fairly done."
So fell the comments on my grateful ear.

Swift in the wake of Joy, and alway near
Walks her sad sister Sorrow. So my brush
Began depicting sorrow, heavy-eyed,
With pallid visage, ere the rosy flush
Upon the beaming face of Joy had dried.
The careful study of long months, it won
Golden opinions ; even bringing forth
That certain sign of merit—a critique

Which set both pieces down as daubs, and weak
As empty heads that sang their praises—so
Proving conclusively the pictures' worth.
These critics and reviewers do not use
Their precious ammunition to abuse
A worthless work. That, left alone, they know
Will find its proper level ; and they aim
Their batteries at rising works which claim
Too much of public notice. But this shot
Resulted only in some noise, which brought
A dozen people, where one came before
To view my pictures ; and I had my hour
Of holding those frail baubles, Fame and Pow'r.
An English Baron who had lived two score
Of his allotted three score years and ten,
Bought both the pieces. He was very kind,
And so attentive, I, not being blind,
Must understand his meaning.
      Therefore, when
He said,
  "Sweet friend, whom I would make my wife,
The 'Joy' and 'Sorrow' this dear hand portrayed
I have in my possession : now resign
Into my careful keeping, and make mine
The joy and sorrow of your future life,"—
I was prepared to answer, but delayed,
Grown undecided suddenly.
      My mind
Argued the matter coolly pro and con,
And made resolve to speed his wooing on

MAURINE.

And grant him favor. He was good and kind ;
Not young, no doubt he would be quite content
With my respect, nor miss an ardent love ;
Could give me ties of family and home ;
And then, perhaps, my mind was not above
Setting some value on a titled name—
Ambitious woman's weakness !
                            Then my art
Would be encouraged and pursued the same,
And I could spend my winters all in Rome.
Love nevermore could touch my wasteful heart
That all its wealth upon one object spent.
Existence would be very bleak and cold,
After long years, when I was gray and old,
With neither home nor children.
                            Once a wife,
I would forget the sorrow of my life,
And pile new sods upon the grave of pain.
My mind so argued ; and my sad heart heard,
But made no comment.
                        Then the Baron spoke,
And waited for my answer. All in vain
I strove for strength to utter that one word
My mind dictated. Moments rolled away—
Until at last my torpid heart awoke,
And forced my trembling lips to say him nay.
And then my eyes with sudden tears o'erran,
In pity for myself and for this man
Who stood before me, lost in pained surprise.

"Dear friend," I cried, "Dear generous friend, forgive
A troubled woman's weakness! As I live,
In truth I meant to answer otherwise.
From out its store, my heart can give you naught
But honor and respect; and yet me-thought
I would give willing answer, did you sue.
But now I know 'twere cruel wrong I planned;
Taking a heart that beat with love most true,
And giving in exchange, an empty hand.
Who weds for love alone, may not be wise:
Who weds without it, angels must despise.
Love and respect together must combine
To render marriage holy and divine;
And lack of either, sure as Fate, destroys
Continuation of the nuptial joys,
And brings regret, and gloomy discontent
To put to rout each tender sentiment.
Nay, nay! I will not burden all your life
By that possession—an unloving wife;
Nor will I take the sin upon my soul
Of wedding where my heart goes not in whole.
However bleak may be my single lot,
I will not stain my life with such a blot.
Dear friend, farewell! the earth is very wide;
It holds some fairer woman for your bride;
I would I had a heart to give to you,
But, lacking it, can only say—adieu!"

He whom temptation never has assailed,
Knows not that subtle sense of moral strength;

When, sorely tried, we waver, but at length,
Rise up and turn away, not having failed.

The Autumn of the third year came and went;
The mild Italian winter was half spent,
When this brief message came across the sea:
"My darling! I am dying. Come to me.
Love, which so long the growing truth concealed,
Stands pale within its shadow. O, my sweet!
This heart of mine grows fainter with each beat—
Dying with very weight of bliss. O, come!
And take the legacy I leave to you,
Before these lips forevermore are dumb,
In life or death. Yours, Helen Dangerfield."

This plaintive letter bore a month old date;
And, wild with fears lest it had come too late,
I bade the old world and new friends adieu,
And with Aunt Ruth, who long had sighed for home,
I turned my back on glory, art, and Rome.

All selfish thoughts were merged in one wild fear
That she for whose dear sake my heart had bled,
Rather than her sweet eyes should know one tear,

Was passing from me; that she might be dead;
And, dying, had been sorely grieved with me,
Because I made no answer to her plea.

"O, ship that sailest slowly, slowly on,
Make haste before a wasting life is gone!
Make haste that I may catch a fleeting breath!
And true in life, be true e'en unto death.

"O, ship sail on! and bear me o'er the tide
To her for whom my woman's heart once died.
Sail, sail, O, ship, for she hath need of me,
And I would know what her last wish may be!
I have been true, so true, through all the past.
Sail, sail, O, ship! I would not fail at last."

So prayed my heart still o'er, and ever o'er,
Until the weary lagging ship reached shore.
All sad with fears that I had come too late,
By that strange source whence men communicate,
Though miles on miles of space between them lie,
I spoke with Vivian: "Does she live? Reply."
The answer came. "She lives, but hasten, friend!
Her journey draweth swiftly to its end."

Ah me! ah me! when each remembered spot,
My own dear home, the lane that led to his—

The fields, the woods, the lake, burst on my sight,
Oh! then, Self rose up in asserting might;
Oh! then, my bursting heart all else forgot,
But those sweet early years of lost delight,
Of hope, defeat, of anguish and of bliss.

I have a theory, vague, undefined,
That each emotion of the human mind,
Love, pain or passion, sorrow or despair,
Is a live spirit, dwelling in the air,
Until it takes possession of some breast;
And, when at length, grown weary of unrest,
We rise up strong and cast it from the heart,
And bid it leave us wholly, and depart,
It does not die, it cannot die; but goes
And mingles with some restless wind that blows
About the region where it had its birth.
And though we wander over all the earth,
That spirit waits, and lingers, year by year,
Invisible, and clothed like the air,
Hoping that we may yet again draw near,
And it may haply take us unaware,
And once more find safe shelter in the breast
It stirred of old with pleasure or unrest.

Told by my heart, and wholly positive,
Some old emotion long had ceased to live;
That, were it called, it could not hear or come,

Because it was so voiceless and so dumb,
Yet, passing where it first sprang into life,
My very soul has suddenly been rife,
With all the old intensity of feeling.
It seemed a living spirit, which came stealing
Into my heart from that departed day;
Exiled emotion, which I fancied clay.

So now into my troubled heart, above
The present's pain and sorrow, crept the love
And strife and passion of a by-gone hour,
Possessed of all their olden might and pow'r.
'Twas but a moment, and the spell was broken
By pleasant words of greeting, gently spoken,
And Vivian stood before us.
                             But I saw
In him the husband of my friend alone,
The old emotions might at times return,
And smould'ring fires leap up an hour and burn;
But never yet had I transgressed God's law,
By looking on the man I had resigned,
With any hidden feeling in my mind,
Which she, his wife, my friend, might not have
        known.

He was but little altered. From his face
The nonchalant and almost haughty grace,—
The lurking laughter waiting in his eyes

The years had stolen, leaving in the place
A settled sadness, which was not despair,
Nor was it gloom, nor weariness, nor care,
But something like the vapor o'er the skies
In Indian summer, beautiful to see,
But spoke of frosts which had been and would be.
There was that in his face which cometh not,
Save when the soul has many a battle fought,
And conquered self, by constant sacrifice.

There are two sculptors, who, with chisels fine,
Render the plainest features half divine.
All other artists strive, and strive in vain,
To picture beauty perfect and complete.
Their statues only crumble at their feet,
Without the master touch of Faith and Pain.
And now his face, that perfect seemed before,
Chiseled by these two careful artists, wore
A look exalted, which the spirit gives
When soul has conquered, and the body lives
Subservient to its bidding.

                In a room
Which curtained out the February gloom,
And, redolent with perfume, bright with flowers
Rested the eye like one of summer's bowers,
I found my Helen, who was less mine now
Than Death's; for on the marble of her brow,

His seal was stamped indelibly.
                                Her form
Was like the slender willow, when some storm
Has stripped it bare of foliage. Her face,
Pale always, now was ghastly in its hue:
And, like two lamps, in some dark, hollow place,
Burned her large eyes, grown more intensely blue.
Her fragile hands displayed each cord and vein,
And on her mouth was that drawn look of pain
Which is not uttered. Yet an inward light
Shone through and made her wasted features bright
With an unearthly beauty; and an awe
Crept o'er me, gazing on her, for I saw
She was so near to Heaven that I seemed
Looking upon the face of one redeemed.

    She turned the brilliant lustre of her eyes
Upon me. She had passed beyond surprise,
Or any strong emotion linked with clay.
But as I glided to her where she lay,
A smile, celestial in its sweetness, wreathed
Her pallid features. "Welcome home!" she breathed.
"Dear hands! dear lips! I touch you and rejoice."
And like the dying echo of a voice
Were her faint tones that thrilled upon my ear.

I fell upon my knees beside her bed;
All agonies within my heart were wed,
While to the aching numbness of my grief,

MAURINE.

Mine eyes refused the solace of a tear,—
The tortured soul's most merciful relief.

Her wasted hand caressed my bended head
For one sad, sacred moment. Then she said
In that low tone so like the wind's refrain,
"Maurine, my own! give not away to pain;
The time is precious. Ere another dawn
My soul may hear the summons and pass on.
Arise sweet sister! rest a little while,
And when refreshed, come hither. I grow weak
With every hour that passes. I must speak
And make my dying wishes known to-night.
Go now." And in the halo of her smile,
Which seemed to fill the room with golden light,
I turned and left her.
                        Later in the gloom
Of coming night, I entered that dim room,
And sat down by her. Vivian held her hand:
And on the pillow at her side, there smiled
The beauteous count'nance of a sleeping child.

"Maurine," spoke Helen, "for three blissful years
My heart has dwelt in an enchanted land;
And I have drank the sweetened cup of joy,
Without one drop of anguish, or alloy.
And so, ere Pain embitters it with gall,
Or sad-eyed Sorrow fills it full of tears,

And bids me quaff, which is the Fate of all
Who linger long upon this troubled way,
God takes me to the realm of Endless Day,
To mingle with His angels, who alone
Can understand such bliss as I have known.
I do not murmur. God has heaped my measure,
In three short years, full to the brim with pleasure;
And, from the fullness of an earthly love,
I pass to th' Immortal arms above,
Before I even brush the skirts of Woe.

"I leave my aged parents here below,
With none to comfort them. Maurine, sweet friend
Be kind to them, and love them, to the end,
Which may not be far distant.
      And I leave
A soul immortal in your charge, Maurine.
From this most holy, sad and sacred eve,
Till God shall claim her, she is yours to keep,
To love and shelter, to protect and guide."
She touched the slumb'ring cherub at her side,
And Vivian gently bore her, still asleep,
And laid the precious burden on my breast.

A solemn silence fell upon the scene.
And when the sleeping infant smiled, and pressed
My yielding bosom with her waxen cheek,
I felt it would be sacrilege to speak,

Such wordless joy possessed me.
                              Oh! at last
This infant, who, in that tear-blotted past,
Had caused my soul such travail, was my own :
Through all the lonely coming years to be
Mine own to cherish—wholly mine alone.
And what I mourned so hopelessly as lost
Was now restored, and given back to me.
The dying voice continued :
                              "In this child
You yet have me, whose mortal life she cost.
But all that was most pure and undefiled,
And good within me, lives in her again.
Maurine, my husband loves me ; yet I know,
Moving about the wide world, to and fro,
And through, and in the busy haunts of men,
Not always will his heart be dumb with woe,
But sometime waken to a later love.
Nay, hush my own ! my soul has passed above
All selfish feelings ! I would have it so.
While I am with the angels, blest and glad,
I would not have you, sorrowing and sad,
In loneliness go mourning to the end.
But, love ! I could not trust to any other
The sacred office of a foster-mother
To this sweet cherub, save my own heart friend.

"Teach her to love her father's name, Maurine,
Where'er he wanders. Keep my mem'ry green

In her young heart, and lead her, in her youth,
To drink from th' eternal fount of Truth ;
Vex her not with sectarian discourse,
Nor strive to teach her piety by force ;
Ply not her mind with harsh and narrow creeds,
Nor frighten her with an avenging God,
Who rules his subjects with a burning rod ;
But teach her that each mortal simply needs
To lean on Christ—to follow where he trod—
To cling to Him with holy faith and trust,
And who so clings, whate'er his creed is, must
Be safe for all Eternity and Time.
Tell her no human life can be sublime
Without this faith. Tell her that God is *Love*—
And love his sceptre, and his throne above ;
That when she sins she wrongs herself, but most
She wrongs the Shepherd of the Heavenly Host,
Who makes her cares and burdens all his own,
And pleads for all her mercies at the throne.

"Let her be free and natural as the flowers,
That smile and nod throughout the summer hours.
Let her rejoice in all the joys of youth,
But first impress upon her mind this truth :
No lasting happiness is e'er attained
Save when the heart some *other* seeks to please.
The cup of selfish pleasures soon is drained,
And full of gall and bitterness the lees.

MAURINE.

Next to her God, teach her to love her land;
In her young bosom light the patriot's flame
Until the heart within her shall expand
With love and fervor at her country's name.
O! do not slight this duty, but inspire
Her woman's soul with patriotic fire.
Upon *her* sons the country yet may call
To rescue freedom from an envious foe.
Let her be strong to send them forth to fall
Rather than see our glorious flag laid low.

" No coward-mother bears a valiant son.
He who lacks valor, better never *be*.
Oh! I were sad in Heaven, knowing one
Of my descendants so forgot his trust,
He did not strike the tyrant to the dust,
Who dared assail the banner of the free!
So teach my child that her blest motherhood
May but result in our loved country's good;
And tell her how our peerless banner waves
Over a million martyrs in their graves.
They gave us freedom! That uncancelled debt
Only the basest craven could forget.
And who remembers, must as sacred hold
Each gleaming star and every waving fold
Of that dear flag—our martyred sires' bequest.

" Maurine, my o'er-taxed strength is waning;
Have heard my wishes, and you will be true

In death as you have been in life, my own!
Now leave me for a little while alone
With him—my husband. Dear love! I shall rest
So sweetly with no care upon my breast.
Good night, Maurine, come to me in the morning."

But lo! the bridegroom with no further warning
Came for her at the dawning of the day.
She heard his voice, and smiled, and passed away
Without a struggle.
                    Leaning o'er her bed
To give her greeting, I found but her clay,
And Vivian bowed beside it. And I said,
" Dear friend! my soul shall treasure thy request,
And when the night of fever and unrest
Melts in the morning of Eternity,
Like a freed bird, then I will come to thee.

I will come to thee in the morning, sweet.
I have been true; and soul with soul shall meet
Before God's throne, and shall not be afraid.
Thou gav'st me trust, and it was not betrayed.

I will come to thee in the morning, dear.
The night is dark. I do not know how near
The morn may be of that Eternal Day;
I can but keep my faithful watch and pray.

I will come to thee in the morning, love;
Wait for me on the Eternal Heights above.
The way is troubled where my feet must climb,
Ere I shall tread the mountain top sublime.

I will come in the morning, O, mine own!
But for a time must grope my way alone,
Through tears and sorrow, till the Day shall dawn,
And I shall hear the summons, and pass on.

I will come in the morning. Rest secure!
My hope is certain and my faith is sure.
After the gloom and darkness of the night
I will come to thee with the morning light."

*   *   *   *   *   *   *

Three peaceful years slipped silently away.
We dwelt together in my childhood's home,
Aunt Ruth and I, and sunny-hearted May.
She was a fair and most exquisite child;
Her pensive face was delicate and mild
Like her dead mother's; but through her dear eyes
Her father smiled upon me, day by day.
Afar in foreign countries did he roam,
Now resting under Italy's blue skies,

And now with Roy in Scotland.
                              And he sent
Brief, friendly letters, telling where he went
And what he saw, addressed to May, or me.
And I would write and tell him how she grew—
And how she talked of papa o'er the sea
In her sweet, baby fashion ; how she knew
His picture in the album ; how each day.
She knelt and prayed the blessed Lord would bring
Her own dear papa back to little May.

It was a warm bright morning in the Spring.
I sat in that same sunny portico,
Where I was sitting seven years ago
When Vivian came. My eyes were full of tears,
As I looked back across the checkered years.
How many were the changes they had brought !
Pain, death,. and sorrow ! but the lesson taught
To my young heart had been of untold worth.
I had learned how to " suffer and grow strong "—
That knowledge which best serves us here on earth,
And brings reward in heaven.
                              Oh ! how long
The years had been since that June morning when
I heard his step upon the walk, and yet
I seemed to hear its echo still.
                              Just then
Down that same path I turned my eyes, tear-wet,
And lo ! the wand'rer from a foreign land

Stood there before me!—holding out his hand
And smiling with those wond'rous eyes of old.

To hide my tears, I ran and brought his child;
But she was shy, and clung to me when told
This was papa, for whom her prayers were said.
She dropped her eyes and shook her little head,
And would not by his coaxing be beguiled,
Or go to him.
            Aunt Ruth was not at home,
And we two sat and talked, as strangers might,
Of distant countries which we both had seen.
But once I thought I saw his large eyes light
With sudden passion, when there came a pause
In our chit-chat, and then he spoke:
                            "Maurine,
I saw a number of your friends in Rome.
We talked of you. They seemed surprised, because
You were not 'mong the seekers for a name.
They thought your whole ambition was for fame."

"It might have been," I answered, "when my heart
Had nothing else to fill it. Now my art
Is but a recreation. I have *this*
To love and live for, which I had not then."
And, leaning down, I pressed a tender kiss
Upon my child's fair brow.

"And yet," he said,
The old light leaping to his eyes again,
"And yet, Maurine, they say you might have wed
A noble Baron! one of many men
Who laid their hearts and fortunes at your feet.
Why won the bravest of them no return?"

I bowed my head, nor dared his gaze to meet.
On cheek and brow I felt the red blood burn,
And strong emotion strangled speech.
        He rose
And came and knelt beside me.
         "Sweet, my sweet!"
He murmured softly, "God in heaven knows
How well I loved you seven years ago.
He only knows my anguish, and my grief,
When your own acts forced on me the belief
That I had been your plaything and your toy.
Yet, from his lips I since have learned that Roy
Held no place nearer than a friend and brother.
And then a faint suspicion, undefined,
Of what had been—was—might be, stirred my mind,
And that great love, I thought died at a blow,
Rose up within me, strong with hope and life.

Before all heaven and the angel mother,
Of this sweet child that slumbers on your heart,
Maurine, Maurine, I claim you for my wife—
Mine own, forever, until death shall part!"

MAURINE.

Through happy mists of upward welling tears,
I leaned, and looked into his beauteous eyes.
"Dear heart," I said, "if she who dwells above
Looks down upon us, from yon azure skies,
She can but bless us, knowing all these years
My soul had yearned in silence for the love
That crowned her life, and left mine own so bleak.
I turned you from me, for her fair, frail sake.
For her sweet child's, and for my own, I take
You back to be all mine, forever more."

Just then the child upon my breast awoke
From her light sleep, and laid her downy cheek
Against her father as he knelt by me.
And this unconscious action seemed to be
A silent blessing, which the mother spoke
Gazing upon us from the mystic shore.

 FINIS.

SOUL OF AMERICA.

SOUL OF AMERICA.

READ AT MADISON, WIS., ON THE TWO HUNDRED AND FIFTY-FIFTH
ANNIVERSARY OF THE PILGRIM LANDING.

And now, when poets are singing
   Their songs of olden days,
And now, when the land is ringing
   With sweet Centennial lays,
My muse goes wandering backward,
   To the groundwork of all these,
To the time when our Pilgrim Fathers
   Came over the winter seas.

The sons of a mighty kingdom,
   Of a cultured folk were they;
Born amidst pomp and splendor,
   Bred in it day by day.

Children of bloom and beauty,
    Reared under skies serene,
Where the daisy and hawthorne blossomed,
    And the ivy was always green.

And yet, for the sake of freedom,
    For a free religious faith,
They turned from home and people,
    And stood face to face with death.
They turned from a tyrant ruler,
    And stood on the new world's shore,
With a waste of waters behind them,
    And a waste of land before.

O, men of a great Republic;
    Of a land of untold worth;
Of a nation that has no equal
    Upon God's round green earth:
I hear you sighing and crying
    Of the hard, close times at hand;
What think you of those old heroes,
    On the rock 'twixt sea and land?

The bells of a million churches
    Go ringing out to-night,
And the glitter of palace windows
    Fills all the land with light;

SOUL OF AMERICA.

And there is the home and college,
   And here is the feast and ball,
And the angels of peace and freedom
   Are hovering over all.

They had no church, no college,
   No banks, no mining stock;
They had but the waste before them,
   The sea, and Plymouth Rock.
But there in the night and tempest,
   With gloom on every hand,
They laid the first foundation
   Of a nation great and grand.

There were no weak repinings,
   No shrinking from what might be,
But with their brows to the tempest,
   And with their backs to the sea,
They planned out a noble future,
   And planted the corner stone
Of the grandest, greatest republic,
   The world has ever known.

O women in homes of splendor,
   O lily-buds frail and fair,
With fortunes upon your fingers,
   And milk-white pearls in your hair:

I hear you longing and sighing
   For some new, fresh delight;
But what of those Pilgrim mothers
   On that December night?

I hear you talking of hardships,
   I hear you moaning of loss;
Each has her fancied sorrow,
   Each bears her self-made cross.
But they, they had only their husbands,
   The rain, the rock, and the sea,
Yet, they looked up to God and blessed Him,
   And were glad because they were free.

O grand old Pilgrim heroes,
   O souls that were tried and true,
With all of our proud possessions
   We are humbled at thought of you:
Men of such might and muscle,
   Women so brave and strong,
Whose faith was fixed as the mountain,
   Through a night so dark and long.

We know of your grim, grave errors,
   As husbands and as wives;
Of the rigid bleak ideas
   That starved your daily lives;

SOUL OF AMERICA.

Of pent-up, curbed emotions,
   Of feelings crushed, suppressed,
That God with the heart created
   In every human breast;

We know of that little remnant
   Of British tyranny.
When you hunted Quakers and witche
   And swung them from a tree;
Yet back to a holy motive,
   To live in the fear of God,
To a purpose, high, exalted,
   To walk where martyrs trod,

We can trace your gravest errors;
   Your aim was fixed and sure,
And e'en if your acts were fanatic,
   We know your hearts were pure.
You lived so near to heaven,
   You over-reached your trust,
And deemed yourselves creators,
   Forgetting you were but dust.

But we with our broader visions,
   With our wider realm of thought,
I often think would be better
   If we lived as our fathers taught.

Their lives seemed bleak and rigid,
    Narrow, and void of bloom;
Our minds have too much freedom,
    And conscience too much room.

They over-reached in duty,
    They starved their hearts for the right
We live too much in the senses,
    We bask too long in the light.
They proved by their clinging to Him
    The image of God in man;
And we, by our love of license,
    Strengthen a Darwin's plan.

But bigotry reached its limit,
    And license must have its sway.
And both shall result in profit
    To those of a later day.
With the fetters of slavery broken,
    And freedom's flag unfurled,
Our nation strides onward and upward,
    And stands the peer of the world.

Spires and domes and steeples,
    Glitter from shore to shore;
The waters are white with commerce,
    The earth is studded with ore;

SOUL OF AMERICA.

Peace is sitting above us,
   And Plenty with laden hand,
Wedded to sturdy Labor,
   Goes singing through the land.

Then let each child of the nation,
   Who glories in being free,
Remember the Pilgrim Fathers
   Who stood on the rock by the sea;
For there in the rain and tempest
   Of a night long passed away,
They sowed the seeds of a harvest
   We gather in sheaves to-day.

MISCELLANEOUS POEMS.

MISCELLANEOUS POEMS.

THE GOSSIPS.

A Rose in my garden, the sweetest and fairest,
   Was hanging her head, through the long golden hours,
And early one morning I saw her tears falling,
   And heard a low gossiping talk in the bowers.
The Fleur-de-leus, a spinster all faded,
   Was telling a Lily what ailed the poor Rose.
"That wild roving bee who was hanging about her,
   Has jilted her squarely, as every one knows."

"I knew, when he came, with his singing and sighing,
   With his airs, and his speeches, so fine, and so sweet,
Just how it would end; but no one would believe me,
   For all were quite ready to fall at his feet."
"Indeed you are wrong," said the Lily belle proudly.
   "I cared nothing for him; he called on me once,

And would have come often, no doubt, if I'd asked
    him,
  But though he was handsome, I thought him a
    dunce."

"Oh, oh, that's not true!" cried the tall Oleander,
  "He has traveled, and seen every flower that grows.
And one who has supped in the garden of Princes,
  We all might have known, would not wed with a
    Rose."
"But wasn't she proud, when she won his attentions,
  And she let him caress her," said sly Mignonette.
"And I used to see it, and blush for her folly,
  But the vain thing believes, he will come to her
    yet."

"I thought he was splendid," said pretty, pert Lark-
    spur,
  "So dark and so grand, with that gay cloak of gold.
But he tried once to kiss me, the impudent fellow,
  And I got offended—I thought him too bold."
"Oh fie!" laughed the Almond, "that does for a story;
  Though I hang down my head, yet I see all that
    goes;
And I saw you reach out, smiling sweet, to detain
    him,
  But he just tapped your cheek, and flew by to the
    Rose."

"He cared nothing for her, he only was flirting,
  To while away time, as I very well knew.
So I turned the cold shoulder on all his advances,
  Because I was certain his heart was untrue."
"Well the Rose is served right for her folly, in trusting
  An oily tongued stranger," quoth proud Columbine,
"I knew what he was, and thought once I would warn her,
  But you know the affair was no matter of mine."

"Oh well!" cried the Peony, shrugging her shoulders,
  "I knew all along, that the bee was a flirt.
But the Rose has been always so praised, and so petted,
  I thought a good lesson would do her no hurt."
Just then came the sound of a love-song, sung sweetly,
  And I saw my sad Rose, lifting up her bowed head.
And the voice of the Gossips was hushed in a moment,
  And the garden was still as the tomb of the dead.
For the dark glossy bee with his cloak o'er his shoulder,
  Came swift o'er the meadow, and kissed the sweet Rose,
And whispered, "My darling, I've roamed the world over,
  But nothing like thee, in the Universe grows."

к

MISCELLANEOUS.

MOTHER LOSS.

If I could clasp my little babe,
  Upon my breast to-night,
I would not mind this blowing wind,
  That shrieketh in affright.
O! my lost babe, my little babe,
  My babe with dreamful eyes,
Thy bed is cold, and night winds bold
  Shriek frightful lullabies.

My breast is softer than the sod.
  This room, with lighted hearth,
Is better place for thy sweet face,
  Than frozen, Mother Earth.
O, my own babe! O, my lost babe!
  O babe with waxen hands,
I want thee so, I miss thee so—
  Come from the silent lands.

No love, but mother-love, that fills
  Each corner of the heart;
No loss, but mother-loss, that chills
  And tears the soul apart.
O, babe! my babe! my helpless babe!
  I miss thy little form,

MISCELLANEOUS.

Would I might creep where thou dost sleep,
  And clasp thee through the storm.

I hold thy pillow to my breast,
  To bring a vague relief.
I sing the songs that soothed thy rest,
  Ah, me! no cheating grief.
My breathing babe, my sighing babe,
  I miss thy plaintive moan.
I cannot hear—thou art not near,
  My little one, my own.

Thy father sleeps; he mourned thy loss,
  But little fathers know
The pain that makes a mother toss
  Through sleepless hours of woe.
My clinging babe! my nursing babe!
  What knows thy father, man,
How my breasts miss thy lips' soft kiss?
  None but a mother can.

Worn out, I sleep! I wake, I weep,
  I sleep—hush, hush, my dear.
Sweet lamb, fear not—O, God! I thought,
  I thought my babe was here.

NOW THE DAYS ARE GROWING LONGER.

Heart of mine, long wrapped in grief,
Look abroad and find relief!
Night, that settled down so soon,
On the very skirts of noon—
Night that lingered, till the morn
In the arms of noon seemed born—
Night so cold, and dark and dreary—
Of its lengthened stay is weary.
Look up, heart, be gladder, stronger,
For the days are growing longer.

Hope seemed buried in the tomb,
With the summer's mirth and bloom.
Sun of joy, and pleasure's light,
All were lost in gloom of night.
Night so long, with tears and sorrow—
Hearts might break ere broke the morrow.
Day so short and night so long—
Fled the bird and hushed the song.
But, my heart, look up, be stronger,
For the days are growing longer.

Sooner o'er the horizon
Creeps the golden sunlight on;

MISCELLANEOUS.

Slower o'er the arching way
Seems to ride the God of day.
Later in the west at night
Linger purple tints of light.
Rise, my heart, rejoice, be stronger,
For the days are growing longer.

By-and-by the night will seem
But a vision-haunted dream;
By-and-by the day will be
Long and glad for you and me.
Laws of recompense shall bring
Days as long and glad in spring
As the nights were long and dreary.
Heart, of tears and gloom a-weary,
Look up; let thy faith be stronger,
For the days are growing longer.

ALL THE WORLD.

All the world is full of babies,
  Sobbing, sighing everywhere;
Looking out, with eyes of terror,
  Beating at the empty air.
Do they see the strife before them,

MISCELLANEOUS.

   That they sob and tremble so?
Oh, the helpless, frightened babies!
   Still they come, and still they go.

All the world is full of children,
   Laughing over little joys,
Sighing over little troubles,
   Fingers bruised and broken toys;
Wishing to be older, larger,
   Weeping at some fancied woe;
Oh, the happy, hapless children!
   Still they come, and still they go.

All the world is full of lovers,
   Walking slowly, whispering sweet,
Dreaming dreams, and building castles
   That must crumble at their feet;
Breaking vows and burning letters,
   Smiling, lest the world shall know!
Oh, the fooling, trusting lovers!
   Still they come, and still they go.

All the world is full of people,
   Hurrying, rushing, pushing by,
Bearing burdens, carrying crosses,
   Passing onward with a sigh;
Some there are with smiling faces,

MISCELLANEOUS.

But with heavy hearts below;
Oh, the sad-eyed, burdened people!
How they come, and how they go!

All the earth is full of sleepers,
　Dust and bones laid there to rest;
This the end that babes and children,
　Lovers, people, find at best.
All their fears and all their crosses,
　All their sorrows wearing so.
Oh, the silent, happy sleepers,
　Sleeping soundly, lying low.

RIVER AND SEA.

Under the light of the silver moon,
　We two sat, when our hearts where young;
The night was warm with the breath of June,
　And loud from the meadow the cricket sung,
　　And darker and deeper, O love, than the sea
　　Were your dear eyes, as they beamed on me.

The moon hung clear, and the night was still;
　The water reflected the glittering skies;

The nightingale sang on the distant hill;
  But sweeter than all was the light in your eyes—
    Your dear, dark eyes, your eyes like the sea,—
    And up from the depths, shone love for me.

My heart, like a river, was mad and wild—
  And a river is not deep, like the sea;
But I said your love was the love of a child,
  Compared with the love that was felt by me.
    A river leaps noisily, kissing the land,
    But the sea is fathomless, deep and grand.

I vowed to love you, for ever and ever;
  I called you cold, on that night in June,
But my fierce love, like a reckless river,
  Dashed on, and away, and was spent too soon;
    While yours—ah, yours was deep, like the sea:
    I cheated you, love, but *you died for me!*

THE "COMMON PEOPLE."

In journeying o'er life's highway
  Where tread so many feet,
And people of all classes,
  Must sometimes pass, or meet,
I think, for friends or neighbors,

MISCELLANEOUS.

If I set out in quest,
I'd choose the "common people,"
I find I like them best.

I'd look for truest heart-friends,
   In all the human race.
Not in the highest station—
   Not in the lowliest place,
But 'mong the common people—
   Who, neither rich nor poor,
Rejoice in some few comforts,
   While toiling on for more.

Some long to dwell 'mong authors—
   With great and gifted men;
I like to listen to them,
   And meet them now and then,
But those who climb for glory
   Dwell so much in the skies,
They cannot read their neighbor's hearts
   For all they may be wise.

I like the common people,
   Who have not wealth, or fame,
Who own no greater riches
   Than a humble home and name.
Among these unknown toilers

MISCELLANEOUS.

In life's great thronged marts—
I find the deepest thinkers—
I find the truest hearts.

Some long to dwell with princes,
  Who breathe but perfumed air;
What with their forms and fashions
  But little comfort's there.
And lives so used to plenty,
  And hearts so bent on "style,"
Can scarcely understand the needs
  Of lowlier lives the while.

To reach "exclusive" circles,
  Some think the height of bliss.
I want a wider kingdom—
  A freer range than this.
Out on the common highways,
  Where common feet have trod,
I feel myself on broader grounds—
  And nearer to my God.

Give me the common people—
  Who walk the common ways.
They've time to think of others' woes
  To sing another's praise.

They dare to laugh in God's fresh air,
  They walk untrammeled—free—
With hearts that feel for more than self,
  These are the friends for me.

OUR BLESSINGS.

Sitting to-day in the sunshine
  That touched me with fingers of love,
I thought of the manifold blessings
  God scatters on earth, from above;
And they seemed, as I numbered them over,
  Far more than we merit, or need,
And all that we lack is the angels
  To make earth a heaven indeed.

The winter brings long, pleasant evenings,
  The spring brings a promise of flowers
That summer breathes into fruition;
  And autumn brings glad, golden hours.
The woodlands re-echo with music,
  The moonbeams ensilver the sea;
There is sunlight and beauty about us,
  And the world is as fair as can be.

But mortals are always complaining!
   Each one thinks his own a sad lot,
And forgetting the good things about him,
   Goes mourning for those he has not.
Instead of the star-spangled heavens,
   We look on the dust at our feet;
We drain out the cup that is bitter,
   Forgetting the one that is sweet.

We mourn o'er the thorn in the flower,
   Forgetting its odor and bloom;
We pass by a garden of blossoms,
   To weep o'er the dust of the tomb.
There are blessings unnumbered about us—
   Like the leaves of the forest they grow;
And the fault is our own—not the Giver's—
   That we have not Eden below.

A FRAGMENT.

Your words came just when needed. Like a breeze,
Blowing and bringing from the wide salt sea
Some cooling spray, to meadow scorched with heat
And choked with dust, and clouds of sifting sand,
That hateful whirlwinds, envious of its bloom,

Had tossed upon it. But the cool sea-breeze
Came laden with the odors of the sea
And damp with spray, that laid the dust and sand
And brought new life and strength to blade and
    bloom.
So words of thine came over miles to me,
Fresh from that mighty sea, a true friend's heart,
And brought me hope, and strength, and swept
    away
The dusty webs that human spiders spun
Across my path. Friend—and the word means much—
So few there are who reach like thee, a hand
Up over all the barking curs of spite,
And give the clasp, when most its need is felt,—
Friend, newly found, accept my full heart's thanks.

MISJUDGED.

Dear friend who hast misjudged me so,
The time may come, when you will know
The wrong you did me, and the pain
You caused the heart you thought so vain.

You deemed it vain, because 'twas light;
Judged by the surface. Out of sight

Were chords no hand had ever woke,
And yet they trembled when you spoke.

What sounds therefrom you might have brought
God only knows, had you not thought
The heart so vain and poor a thing
That all alike could make it sing.

'Tis true it gives a lightsome air
To all who touch it, here or there.
Harps strung alway for music so
Must needs respond when breezes blow.

But there are better chords that would
Have answered to your touch for good.
Chords full and deep, and rich and grand,
Worthy the master's withheld hand.

MISCELLANEOUS.

THE MANIAC.

I saw them sitting in the shade ;
   The long green vines hung over
But could not hide the gold-haired maid
   And Earl—my blue-eyed lover.
His arm was clasped so close, so close,
   Her eyes were softly lifted,
While his eyes drank the cheek of rose,
   And breast like snow-flakes drifted.

A strange noise sounded in my brain :
   I was a guest unbidden.
I stole away—but came again
   With two steels snugly hidden.
I stood behind them ; close they kissed
   While eye to eye was speaking.
I aimed my steels, and neither missed
   The heart I sent it seeking.

There were two death shrieks, mingled so
   It seemed like one voice crying.
I laughed. It was such bliss, you know,
   To hear, and see them dying.
I laughed and shouted, while I stood
   Above the lovers, gazing

Upon the little rills of blood,
   And in the eyes fast glazing.

It was such joy to see the rose
   Fade from her cheek forever;
To know the lips he kissed so close
   Could answer never—never.
To see his arm grow stiff and cold,
   And know it could not fold her;
To know that while the world grew old,
   His eyes could not behold her.

A crowd of people thronged about,
   Brought thither by my laughter;
I gave one last triumphant shout—
   And darkness followed after.
That was a thousand years ago—
   Each hour I live it over,
For here, just out of reach, you know,
   She lies, with Earl, my lover.

They lie there, staring, staring so,
   With great glazed eyes, to taunt me.
Will no one bury them down low
   Where they shall cease to haunt me?
He kissed *her* lips, not mine. The flowers
   And vines hung all around them.

Sometimes I sit and laugh for hours,
  To think just how I found them.

And then sometimes I stand and shriek
  In agony of terror,
Thinking the red warms in her cheek—
  Then laugh loud at my error.
My cheek was all too pale, he thought;
  He deemed hers far the brightest;
Ha! but my dagger touched a spot
  That made *her* cheek turn whitest.

THE CHANGE.

She leaned out into the soft June weather;
  With her long loose tresses the night breeze played
Her eyes were as blue as the bells on the heather;
  Oh, what is so fair as a fair young maid!

She folded her hands, like the leaves of a lily.
  "My life," she said, "is a night in June,
Fair and quiet, and calm and stilly;
  Bring me a change, O changeful moon!

Who would drift on a lake forever?
   Young hearts weary—it is not strange,
And sigh for the beautiful bounding river;
   New moon, true moon, bring me a change!"

The rose that rivaled her maiden blushes
   Dropped from her breast, at a stranger's feet:
Only a glance; but the hot blood rushes
   To mantle a fair face, shy and sweet.

To and fro, while the moon is waning,
   They walk, and the stars shine on above;
And one is in earnest, and one is feigning—
   Oh, what is so sweet, as sweet young love?

A young life crushed, and a young heart broken,
   A bleak wind blows through the lonely bower,
And all that remains of the love vows spoken
   Is the trampled leaf of a faded flower.

The night is dark, for the moon is failing—
   And what is so pale, as a pale old moon!
Cold is the wind through the tree tops wailing—
   Woe that the change should come so soon!

RELICS.

This is her crochet-work, just as she left it,
The spool, with the needle caught into its side,
And the edging wound up in a neat little bundle;
She had been knitting, the day that she died.

This is her dress, hanging here in the closet,
The last one she hung here; 'twill never be moved;
She wore it the morn of the day that she sickened,
And it constantly speaks of the maiden we loved.

This is her glove, lying here on the table,
Bearing the marks of her fingers, you see;
Just as she tossed it aside, I shall leave it;
It is more than a diamond, or topaz, to me.

This is the last book her eye ever glanced in,
The blue ribbon mark shows how far she had read.
That morn, she was better, she said, and was reading
Aloud; and at a dusk, the same day, she was dead.

This is a letter: begun, but not finished;
Her head ached, she said, and she laid it aside.
And these little relics, so sacredly guarded,
Are all that are left of the dear girl that died.
1869.

THE DREAMER.

She sits in the winter gloaming
    And reads by the waning light
The tender words of her lover
    From the page of creamy white;
And over her cheek, like sunbeams
    Over the morning skies,
The blushes of virgin passion
    Billow, and break, and rise.

She dreams of a summer coming;
    Of a fragrant summer night;
Of a wreath of orange blossoms,
    And a trailing robe of white;
Of lingering, passionate kisses—
    Of music, bells and mirth,
And the light of joys celestial
    Upon the green-clad earth.

O happy twilight muser,
    O heart like a fluttering dove,
Dream on in the winter gloaming
    Your bright, brief dream of love.
Dream out the blissful romance
    Your young life cannot know,

MISCELLANEOUS.

For never the kiss of bridegroom
   Shall fall on that brow of snow.

Dream on of a summer coming,
   O young heart fond and true,
But the arms of a ghostly lover
   Are reaching out for you.
He is drawing nearer, nearer,
   With a robe that you must wear,
And a cluster of white tube-roses
   To place in your auburn hair.

Never the orange blossoms—
   And the robe is white, but plain,
With never a flounce or ruffle,
   And no long, queenly train.
And the bells will be tolling, tolling,
   And there will be gloom and tears,
And only the sounds of sorrow,
   When the bridegroom Death appears.

But dream out your dream, my maiden'
   You have the sweetest part,
And death shall come and claim you,
   Ere sorrow strikes your heart.
Better the pale tube-roses,
   And the robe with never a fold,

Than the faded orange blossoms,
   Trampled, and stained, and old,

Better the fair young maiden,
   Buried in all her bloom,
Than the life of a hopeless woman,
   With her heart in a living tomb.
Better to read the prologue,
   And never another page,
Than to wait and finish the story,
   In a querulous, bleak old age.

So dream in the winter twilight;
   You have the sweetness now;
And the bridegroom Death shall claim you
   Ere sorrow marks your brow.

NORINE.

"What shall I wear to the ball, MaBelle,
   What shall I wear to the ball?
Make me fairer than tongue can tell—
   Make me the fairest of all."

MISCELLANEOUS.

"Fair? You are always fair Norine—
  Ever and always fair.
Born to be star of the night, and queen,
  Whatever you choose to wear!"

"But I must be fairer than ever, MaBelle,
  Fairer than ever before;
That *he* may approve, with eyes of love
  And worship forever more."

"*He?* It has ever been *they*, Norine!
  What! you who tread on hearts
And laugh at their pain, and call love vain—
  You caught at last by its arts?"

"Hush, hush! I have found my king MaBelle,
  I am reading the story old.
Oh, make me so fair, that his lips must swear,
  The love that his eyes have told."

"Down to the carriage swept Norine—
  Away she rode to the ball.
Of all the maidens the stars had seen—
  She was the fairest of all."

"Oh, put these baubles away MaBelle,
  And help me to get undressed.
How weary I am dear, none can tell—
  I am longing so for rest."

"What! Home from the ball so soon, Norine,
  And pale as the robe you wear?
And how could the revelers spare their Queen,
  And say! did he think you fair?"

"Hush, hush! he was there with his bride, MaBelle.
  He was there with his bride at the ball,
We met, in the crowd, and he smiled and bowed,
  And I stole away from them all."

"Ah! God is just, and He reigns, Norine!
  Aye! bury your face, and weep;
Your fault, you know—we reap as we sow—
  Go now to your troubled sleep."

MISCELLANEOUS.

FLOWN AWAY.

In the Linden tree the live-long day,
    A mother robin has sat and cried.
"Lonely, lonely," she seems to say—
    Sitting her empty nest beside.
There's a dreary void in her aching breast,
    For in the dawning, dim and grey,
Her wee birds rose from the downy nest,
    And flew to the forest—away, away.

I sit at my window, sad and alone,
    And my heart echoes the robin's cry;
For out of the nest my birds have flown—
    And we are so lonely—my heart and I.
We listen in vain for the sound of feet
    Ringing and tripping from stair to hall,
In vain for the echo of voices sweet;
    dreary silence is over all.

In a glimmer of gems, and a sheen of white
    With the orange wreath on her snowy brow
My wee bird Maud went out last night,
    And I am alone in the old home now.
Alone with the memories sweet and sad,
    That flit like spirits from room to room,

Bright young faces, and voices glad,
   Lips of sweetness and cheeks of bloom.

Nothing but ghosts. The mother bird
   Just now started with joyful screams,
For something, she thought, in the old nest stirred
   'Twas only the ghostly feet of dreams.
We toiled for our birdies day by day,
   We shielded them ever with our own breasts,
Only to see them fly away,
   And make their homes in other nests.

They follow the path our feet have trod—
   I say it over, and over, and sigh,
" 'Tis the law of heaven—the will of God,"
   Yet we are so lonely—the bird and I.
Nests must be builded, and homes be made,
   The world must keep up its strength and might,
Yet two lone hearts in the gathering shade,
   Wish that their birdies were back, to-night.

THE WORLD.

Alone in my cozy chamber—
　Yet I cannot read or write,
For the spell of the past is upon me
　And sways my heart to-night.
My lecture lies half completed ;
　My books hold many a gem
That is mine, I know, for the taking—
　But to-night I turn from them.

world ! do you brand forever
　The hearts that have once been thine?
Are they cursed with the curse of longing
　Who have once knelt at thy shrine?
I drank my fill of thy pleasures—
　Drank till the sweets were sour,
And I counted the cost—and the charm was lost
　And I freed myself from thy power.

I said, " I will seek for knowledge !
　I will climb to higher ground.
For there are on the hills of Wisdom,
　True pleasure, alone, is found."
So here with my books and studies,

With my flute, and violin,
I spend the days to my profit—
And at eve, some friend drops in.

And we chat o'er our cozy supper,
   Of Science, Progress, Art,
And I feel with a glow of pleasure,
   In these I have earned a part.
I shall leave some good behind me—
   I have worked for God, and man;
I have dug some truths from the mine of thought,
   And aided an All-wise plan.

And yet—and yet—ah Heaven!
   There come to me times like this,
When I thirst for empty pleasures—
   For the world and its cheating bliss.
I long with sensuous longing
   For the perfume, glitter, and glow,
That drugged the reason and senses,
   And set the spirits aflow.

Oh to be back this moment—
   For an hour of the old delight!
Oh for the strains of the "Danube,"
   For the revel and ball, to-night!
Oh for the feast, and the banquet,

MISCELLANEOUS.

The toast and the maddening wine!
Oh world! do you curse forever,
  A heart that has once been thine?

A POEM.

READ BEFORE THE ST. ANDREW'S SOCIETY, JANUARY 8, 1875.

Who sings of Scotland's glories
  Can sing in no new strain.
The oft repeated stories
  Can but be told again.
We know its hills are rugged,
  Its valleys fair and green,
With nodding copes and verdant slopes,
  And the "Silver Tay" between.

We know it's the land of beauty,
  For, in its hapless queen,
It gave us the fairest woman
  The world has ever seen.
Its daughters are like its valleys,
  So fresh and blooming fair,
While its sons are like its mountains,
  That rise in their grandeur there.

MISCELLANEOUS.

We know it's the land of genius,
   That it fathered minds of worth,
And fed, by its wild, romantic scenes,
   The master brains of earth ;
It gave us the songs of Ossian,
   Of Campbell, Burns and Scott,
And the veins of England's greatest bard
   With Scottish blood were fraught.

We know it's the land of heroes,
   Of sturdy warriors bold :
The brave and glorious Wallace,
   Pendragon, famed of old,
Douglass, and Bruce, and Malcolm,
   All heroes grand and strong,
Whose deeds are told in story,
   And sung in the poet's song.

We know how its noisy bagpipe,
   With its clamor wild and shrill,
Has played alone on the battle field,
   When horns and drums were still.
How once, on the shores of India,
   And again at Quebec, its blast
Roused up the troops disheartened,
   And saved the day at last.

We know its creed is simple,
   Its faith a living joy,
Alike to the holy man at kirk
   And to the shepherd boy.
And better than gorgeous temples,
   Than mass and organ blast
Is the faith they learn at the fireside
   And keep in their hearts to the last.

And so, in creed and in beauty,
   In romance, glory, worth,
In song and martial music,
   Old Scotland leads the earth.

Who sings of Scotland's glories
   Can sing of nothing new—
Can but re-tell the stories
   The whole world knows are true,
And, though its sons may wander
   To many a distant shore,
A Scot's a Scot forever,
   And but loves his land the more.

LOST.

You left me with the autumn time :
   When winter stripped the forest bare,
Then dressed it in his spotless rime ;
   When frosts were lurking in the air
You left me here and went away ;
The winds were cold ; you could not stay.

You sought a warmer clime, until
   The South wind, artful maid, should break
The winter's trumpets, and should fill
   The air with songs of birds, and wake
The sleeping blossoms on the plain,
And make the brooks to flow again.

I thought the winter desolate,
   And all times felt a sense of loss.
I taught my longing heart to wait,
   And said, "when spring shall come across
The hills, with blossoms in her track,
Then she, our loved one, will come back."

And now the hills with grass and moss
   The spring, with cunning hands, has spread.

MISCELLANEOUS.

And yet I feel my grievous loss.
   My heart will not be comforted,
But crieth daily, "where is she
You promised should come back to me?"

O Love! where are you? Day by day
   I seek to find you, but in vain.
Men point me to a grave, and say:
   "There is her bed, upon the plain."
But though I see no trace of you,
   I cannot think their words are true.

You were too sweet to wholly pass
   Away from earth, and leave no trace;
You were too fair to let the grass
   Grow rank and tall above your face.
Your voice, that mocked the robin's trill,
I cannot think is hushed and still.

I thought I saw your golden hair,
   One day, and reached to touch a strand;
I found but yellow sunbeams there;
   The bright rays fell aslant my hand
And seemed to mock, with lights and shades,
The silken meshes of your braids.

Again, I thought I saw your hand
    Wave, as if beckoning to me;
I found 'twas but a lily, fanned
    By the cool zephyrs from the sea.
O, Love! I find no trace of you;
I wonder if their words *were* true?

One day I heard a singing voice—
    A burst of music, trill on trill,
It made my very soul rejoice;
    My heart gave an exultant thrill.
I cried, "O heart, we've found her—hush!"
But no—'twas the silver-throated thrush.

And once I thought I saw your face,
    And wild with joy I ran to you;
But found, when I had reached the place,
    'Twas but a blush-rose, bathed in dew.
Ah, Love! I think you *must* be dead;
And I believe the words they said.

MISCELLANEOUS.

UPON THE WAY.

For pausing on the way awhile
To make some other pilgrim smile,
E'en though it puts us back a mile,
   We've time enough for that, my friend.
The day is long, and bright, and glad;
To stop a bit and cheer the sad,
   Will never hinder in the end.

To loiter ever now and then,
To answer bitter words of men,
And give for scoff a scoff again,
   We have not time for that, my friend.
The night is nearer than we know;
To stop and deal out blow for blow
   Will hinder sorely in the end.

For pausing sometimes on the way,
And seeking some who've gone astray,
Restoring them to light and day,
   We've time enough to spare, my friend.
To stop and lift some other's load,
Will lighten ours upon the road,
   And can but help us in the end.

To linger by the road and wait
Some season to retaliate
For every spiteful act of hate,
   We have no time to spare, my friend.
To stone each barking dog we hear,
To kill each insect flying near,
   Will only hinder in the end.

To sum it up in words like these,
We've time to praise, but none to tease;
We've time to soothe, and time to please,
   But none to grieve or wound, my friend.
And if we wisely spend each day,
We'll find true pleasure on the way,
   And God will help us to the end.

MY VISION.

Wherever my feet may wander,
   Wherever I chance to be,
There comes, with the coming of even-time
   A vision sweet, to me.
I see my mother sitting
   In the old familiar place,
And she rocks to the tune her needles sing,
   And thinks of an absent face.

MISCELLANEOUS.

I can hear the roar of the city
   About me now as I write;
But over an hundred miles of snow
   My thought-steeds fly to-night,
To the dear little cosy cottage,
   And the room where mother sits,
And slowly rocks in her easy chair
   And thinks of me as she knits.

Sometimes with the merry dancers,
   When my feet are keeping time,
And my heart beats high, as young hearts will,
   To the music's rythmic chime,
My spirit slips over the distance
   Out of the glitter and whirl,
To my mother who sits, and rocks, and knits,
   And thinks of her "little girl."

When I listen to voices that flatter,
   And smile, as women do,
To whispered words that may be sweet,
   But are not always true,
I think of the sweet, quaint picture
   Afar in quiet ways,
And I know one smile of my mother's eyes
   Is better than all their praise.

And I know I can never wander
   Far from the path of right,
Though snares are set for a woman's feet
   In places that seem most bright.
For the vision is with me always,
   Wherever I chance to be,
Of mother sitting, rocking and knitting,
   Thinking and praying for me.

RESIGNED.

My babe was moaning in its sleep;
   I leaned and kissed it where it lay;
My pain was such I could not weep.
   Oh, would God take my child away?
He had so many 'round his throne—
If He took mine—I stood alone!

I held my child upon my knee;
   It looked up with its father's eyes,
Who, ere the infant came to me,
   Had journeyed homeward to the skies.
But through those eyes, so sad and mild,
I found my husband, in my child.

MISCELLANEOUS.

It was such comfort, night and day,
   To watch its slumber—feel its breath—
And slow—so slow—it pined away,
   I heard not th' approach of Death
Until he stood close at my side,
   And then my soul within me died.

I clasped my babe with sudden moan,
   I cried, "My sweet, thou shalt not go
To join the children 'round the Throne,
   For I have need of thee below.
If God takes thee, I am bereft—
No hope or joy or comfort left."

My babe looked pleading in my face;
   It seemed my husband's eyes instead,
And his voice sounded in the place,
   "I want my child in heaven," it said.
The infant raised its little hands,
And seemed to reach toward heavenly lands.

The tears that had refused to flow,
   Came welling upward from my heart;
I sobbed, "My child, then thou may'st go,
   Thy angel father bids us part.
I know in all that heavenly place
He ne'er looked on so sweet a face.

"He does not even know thy name,
   And all these months, he's longed for thee.
How could I so forget his claim—
   And strive to keep thee at my knee?
Go child—my child—and give him this—
In one the wife's and mother's kiss."

My baby smiled, and seeming slept.
   Its hand grew cold within my own.
Not wholly sad the tears I wept,
   For though I was indeed alone,
My babe I knew was safe at rest
   Upon its angel father's breast.

TWO JUNES.

She sat, with her young-old face,
And her form of blighted grace,
And looked with her sad, unseeing eyes,
On the green June earth and the blue June skies;
And she moaned and sang in an undertone,
A song of Junes to her heart alone.

"There was a June, Oh, ages past!
   When the days were flooded with golden light.

And the moments flitted away too fast,
  My heart was so happy from morn till night.
That was the June of '74.
  Strange how this can be '75!
It is fully a hundred years ago
  Since that sweet June was alive.

Why, then I had scarcely wept a tear,
  And now I have wept my tears all dry;
One could not weep so much in a year—
  It must be longer since June went by.
Yet this is '75, they say,
  And that was '74, I know;
But it seems, on looking back to-day,
  Ages and ages ago.

Why, then I was just in my youth's glad prime;
  And now I am old in heart and face.
Could one grow old in a year's short time,
  And lose all beauty and youth and grace?
Yet this, they say, is '75,
  And I know it was '74 when
He—yes, I *must* have been alive
  One hundred years since then.

Love and laughter made all things fair;
  Joy sat by me with folded wing;

Now each day is a blank despair—
  How could a year change everything?
Some one has figured the calendar wrong—
  This must be 1975,
And 101 years have dragged along
  Since that sweet June was alive."

BLESS THE BABIES.

Bless the little babies!
  Oh, they make the home,
Keeping husband evenings,
  Time he used to roam.
Boon companions miss him—
  Cards have lost their charms;
There he sits contented,
  Baby in his arms.

Bless the little babies!
  Oh they strip the heart
Of all false allurements,
  By their native art.
Once the belle, a mother;
  Fashion, fol-de-rol;
Selfish whims that spoiled her,
  Vanish one and all.

Bless the little babies!
  Bridging many a breach,
'Twixt the wife and husband,
  Binding each to each.
Husband stops his growling,
  Warmed by baby's smiles;
Wife forgets her grievance,
  Watching baby's wiles.

Bless the little babies!
  Shame upon the wives
Ruled by Self, and Fashion,
  Living barren lives.
Out upon the practice,
  Murder—nothing less,
Of the scores of women
  God had meant to bless.

Bless the little babies!—
  Blessings, few or many,
Pity on the household
  Never counting any.
It is like a garden
  Where there are no flowers;
Bless the pretty blossoms,
  Filling happy bowers.

SLANDER.

A whispered word from a woman's lips,
As a slimy snake through a fair field slips;
A shrug, or a glance, like a poison dart
Aimed from behind at a creature's heart.

The snake glides stealthily on its way,
And a laughing child is killed at play;
The whispered word gains force, and lo!
A fame is black that was white as snow.

Dead in her track falls the bounding hind,
Slain by the arrow shot from behind.
The shrug and the glance have gained apace,
And the light goes out of a fair young face.

Pull out the dart! Does the hind awake?
Does it bring back life, though you kill the snake?
Prove the tale false! yet the heart is wrung.
Oh, the curse of God on a slanderous tongue.

THE VOLUPTUARY.

Oh, I am sick of love reciprocated!
   Of hopes fulfilled—ambitions gratified.
Life holds no thing to be anticipated,
   And I am sad from being satisfied.

The eager joy, felt climbing up the mountain,
   Has left me, now the highest peak is gained.
The crystal spray that fell from Fame's fair fountain
   Was sweeter than the waters were, when drained.

The gilded apple which the world calls Pleasure,
   And which I purchased with my youth and strength,
Pleased me a moment. But the empty treasure
   Lost all its lustre, and grew dim at length.

And love all glowing with a golden glory,
   Delighted me a season with its tale.
It pleased the longest. But at last the story
   So oft repeated to my heart, grew stale.

I lived for self, and all I sought was given.
   I have had all, and now am sick of bliss.

No other punishment designed by heaven,
  Could strike me half so forcibly as this.

I feel no sense of aught but enervation,
  In all the joys my selfish aims have brought.
And have no wish but for annihilation,
  Since that would give me freedom from all thought.

Oh, blest is he, who has some aim defeated,
  Some mighty loss to balance all his gain!
For him there is a hope not yet completed,
  For him life yet has draughts of joy and pain.

And, cursed is he, who knows no balked ambition,
  No hopeless hope, no loss beyond repair.
But sick and sated with complete fruition,
  Knows not the pleasure even of Despair.

PRINCE OF THE WALTZERS.

Listlessly up the stairway,
  And listlessly through the hall
With her bright smile fled, and her roses dead,
  Creeps the belle of the ball;
It is only the hour of midnight;
  Why did she hasten so,
And leave the Prince of the Waltzers
  To seek for her, high and low?

Alone in her quiet chamber,
  She flings off flowers and pearls,
And she tosses her robe in the corner,
  And takes out the comb from her curls.
And her cheek is whiter than lilies,
  And the tears they fall and fall;
With the gloom on her brow, would you know her
      now,
  For the brilliant belle of the ball?

To and fro in her chamber
  She paces with restless feet;
She fancies she hears the dancers,
  And the music beat and beat.

She can hear the beautiful Danube,
    And her tears fall down like rain,
For she knows the Prince of the Waltzers
    In seeking for her in vain.

Why did she leave the ballroom?
    Because she dared not stay,
Lest on the sweet, sweet music's beat
    Her soul should be carried away.
For how can a woman be guarded
    Against an alluring glance,
Or the light caress of a soft hand-press,
    In the swift, bewildering dance.

Oh why was the world created,
    If never a soul is glad?
And why should love be given
    If only to make us sad?
And why should the Prince of Waltzers
    Be tied to a sickly wife?
And why should the belle of the ballroom
    Love him better than life?

Over and over, these problems
    Go surging through her brain,
While afar the Prince of the Waltzers
    Is seeking for her in vain.

And not till over the mountains
   The rays of the morning creep,
Does the brilliant belle of the season
   Sink into a troubled sleep.

Oh, weep in your slumber, my lady!
   You shall weep more bitterly yet.
It is ever so—there are tears and woe
   For those who their God forget.
You live to triumph and conquer;
   You are belle of the feast and the ball;
But the sweets in the cup—you have drained them,
   And now you must drink the gall.

AN OLD MAN'S VIEW.

   We've had no trouble, life and I,
   Since Love shook hands, and said good-by;
   I mean that fierce young love of youth,
   So praised by poets, but in truth
   An imp, by wicked fairies sent
   To fill the heart with discontent.

   What time he occupied my breast,
   He racked me with a wild unrest.

I could not sleep, I could not toil;
He chilled my blood, and made it boil.
He tossed me to a dizzy height,
Then dragged me to the depths of night.

One moment life would seem so sweet,
I skimmed the earth with winged feet.
The next, 'twas like a cruel weight,
And all the world was desolate.
Love kept me in such constant strife,
I had no comfort with my life.

Now, since he's ceased to be my guest
My heart beats calmly in my breast.
No longer burned by fears, or pains,
My blood flows calmly through my veins,
A healthy tide; and brings me sleep,
From which I do not wake to weep.

I relish labor, and my food.
All day I'm in a happy mood.
My books, my friends, my toils, bring joy
And calm content without alloy.
I've had love's worst, and best, you see,
And know he holds no more for me.

Some hearts there are God-fashioned so,
Love can come in but once, you know.
And such a one was given me.
And others by the score I see
Wherein love ever comes and goes ;
I'm glad I have not one of those,

For such know never that sweet peace,
Which comes but when love's visits cease.
No longer ridged by fear or doubt,
A level plain life stretches out,
Just sweetly lighted to the end
By star of faith, and smile of friend.

DYING YEAR.

O year wherein all sorrows have been crowded,
  O year more solemn than all other years,
O year whose skies from first to last were clouded
  O year adrip with salt and bitter tears,
You die ! and I could shout aloud for gladness,
  To see you die, cold 1875.
It is the sole emotion, save of sadness,
  My heart has felt since first you were alive.

The very moment that you sprang to being,
   You seemed to owe me bitterness and spite.
And now I'm filled with mirth and laughter seeing
   How low you lie, and in such humbled plight.
From January until late December,
   Through all the months of wind, and storm and rain,
You gave me little that I can remember
   With any feeling but regret and pain.

You made me weep, till all my soul was flooded,
   But sent new hopes, ere reason quite was lost.
And these you left me till they sweetly budded,
   And then you nipped them with a killing frost.
You would not even let me have a summer,
   But sent cold rains to fill it full of gloom.
Whoe'er, whate'er, may be this unknown comer,
   I shall rejoice to see you in your tomb.

How cold you are, and how you shake, and shiver,
   I love that wind, that howls about your bed.
I love to see your palsied limbs a-quiver!
   And know so soon you will be cold and dead.
O murderer, who slew my friends and left me,
   Liar, who promised, but who never gave,
Thief, who of happiness and hope bereft me,
   I spit upon your coffin and your grave.

PLEA TO SCIENCE.

O Science reaching backward through the distance,
    Most earnest child of God,
Exposing all the secrets of existence,
    With thy divining rod,
I bid thee speed up to the heights supernal,
    Clear thinker, ne'er sufficed ;
Go seek and bind the laws and truths eternal,
    But leave me Christ.

Upon the vanity of pious sages
    Let in the light of day.
Break down the superstitions of all ages—
    Thrust bigotry away ;
Stride on, and bid all stubborn foes defiance ;
    Let truth and reason reign.
But I beseech thee, O Immortal Science,
    Let Christ remain.

What can'st thou give to help me bear my crosses,
    In place of Him, my Lord?
And what to recompense for all my losses,
    And bring me sweet reward?
Thou couldst not with thy clear, cold eyes of reason,
    Thou couldst not comfort me

Like one who passed through that tear-blotted season,
    In sad Gethsemane!

Through all the weary, wearing hour of sorrow,
    What word that thou hast said,
Would make me strong to wait for some to-morrow
    When I should find my dead?
When I am weak, and desolate, and lonely—
    And prone to follow wrong?
Not thou, O Science—Christ, my Saviour, only
    Can make me strong.

Thou art so cold, so lofty, and so distant,
    Though great my need might be,
No prayer, however constant and persistent,
    Could bring thee down to me.
Christ stands so near, to help me through each hour,
    To guide me day by day.
O Science, sweeping all before thy power—
    Leave Christ, I pray.

MISCELLANEOUS.

TWO SEASONS.

He waited at the trysting place,
　While she tripped o'er the meadow
A girlish creature full of grace,
　Whose step dispelled the shadows.
The earth lay in the arms of June,
　She said, "All life is beauty;
The world is set in perfect tune;
　To live and love is duty."

Her lover called her from the glade;
　She loitered on unheeding,
So used to love, the tyrant maid
　Held lightly lovers' pleading.
"The days are long and sweet," she
　"Love only fills one measure;
I'll drink of every other draught,
　And taste of love at pleasure."

She gazed across the wintry way,
　The trysting place was lonely,
She thought, "How I would fly to-d[ay]
　If he were waiting only."
The earth lay clasped in Winter's hol[d]
　She said, "The world is dreary,

My life is very bleak and cold,
   My heart is very weary."

The voice that called her from the glade,
   No more did echoes waken,
And losing love, the saddened maid,
   Prized highly what was taken.
"The days are long and lone," she sighed,
   "And pain fills every measure,
In vain all all other joys I've tried,
   Love lost, earth holds no pleasure."

Then leaning with her face bowed on her knees,
   She sobbed and sighed out lonely words like these:

"If he could know how I am sitting, lonely,
   Shunning all others since I have not him;
If he could know my heart enshrines one only,
   For whom my longing eyes are ofttimes dim,
He would come back across the weary space,
Come with the olden lovelight on his face.

If he could know how I repent in sorrow,
   The idle words that drove him from my side,
Though leagues away, he would come back to-morrow,
   And all my sad life would be glorified.

And were you never lonely on the way?
Sometimes you seem so near, so near, to me,
And then I say, "Ah no, it cannot be.
She does not dwell on any distant shore,
But lives, and moves beside me ever more."

What have you seen in all this time, my loved one,
   With those young eyes, so tender, calm, and clear.
Immortal lands of undulating beauty—
   Jehovah throned, and all his angels near?
Was such the heaven that burst upon your sight,
And were your eyes so dazzled by the light,
You have not once looked back on earth to see,
How goes the battle of this life with me?

What have you done through all the days, my brave
      one?
   An idle hour on earth you never knew.
And all the joys of heaven could not content you,
   Unless your hands had some good work to do.
You would grow weary even there of rest.
Some round of labors ever pleased you best.
What are they now, which all your days employ
And give you constant and eternal joy?

What is the form you wear in heaven, my fair one?
   That queenly shape—that large and beauteous eye,

The long bright hair that swept about your shoulders,
  Were not these reproduced again on high?
Or were they left down in the grave with death,
And what remains—intangible as breath?
Or did you take some other shape, more fair?
And what name do they call you, over there?

Oh answer me, my loved one, and my lost one!
  Why, once I could not ask you anything,
But you replied in words of gracious sweetness—
  Now you are deaf to all my questioning.
O my dead friend make answer I implore!
As days go by, I miss you more and more.
The place you held, no other friend can fill.
Lean down and whisper that you love me still.

THE CHERUB YEAR.

O infant New Year! free from stain,
  With spotless heart and wide, pure eyes,
Young king of all the broad domain
  That stretches underneath yon skies,
Know ye how great is thy estate?
  Know ye the glory that ye wear?
Does thy young heart appreciate
  The noble title that ye bear?

Thy great, great sire was '76,
  Whose fame can never more grow dim.
Of ninety-nine direct in line,
  Thou only, child, wert named for him.
He was the monarch of the world!
  He was a warrior bold and free.
Our starry banner he unfurled,
  And waved it over land and sea.

He broke the chain of Tyranny,
  And dared to boldly take the land
And wed the maiden Liberty,
  And make her Queen of all the land.
O Cherub 1876,
  Go think upon thy great sire's fame.
Come day or night,—come bloom or blight,—
  Strive to be worthy of his name.

SWEETHEART.

Sweetheart, sweeter than all other,
(And I have had many another,)
    Come here, please.
Come and sit you down beside me;
Chat or gossip, praise or chide me,
    Scold or tease.

MISCELLANEOUS.

Only talk, so I can listen ;
Let me see those dear eyes glisten ;
    Let me gaze
On that sweet face, like a flower,
That shall hold me with its power
    All my days.

I have wooed, as men do often ;
Scores of eyes have I made soften.
    But, my dove—
Never any breathing woman—
Never any creature human
    Won my love ;
Won, and kept it still increasing,
Never lessening or ceasing
    As you do.
Never was my heart love-laden,
Though I've smiled on many a maiden,
    Save for you.

I'd a love for every season.
Loved for this and for that reason—
    Fancy's laws ;
Many a maid I've loved for pleasure ;
You I love the fullest measure,
    Just—because.
Maids took pains to always please me ;

MISCELLANEOUS.

You, although you plague and tease me,
    I adore.
Those I loved, to keep in fashion;
You I give by heart's best passion,
    Evermore.

Foolish maid, is she refusing
Since she's not a heart's first choosing?
    For I hold
He who roams the wide world over
Makes at last the truest lover,
    Good as gold.
All the gems of earth comparing,
When he takes one for his wearing,
    His to be,
He knows how to guard his treasure;
Sweet, my latest, dearest pleasure,
    Come to me.

MY LADY.

My lady sits in her rose-hued room,
   And looks from her window on tropical bowers;
Her life is a poem of beauty and bloom,
   And she spends her days like the hot-house flowers.

She stars with fortunes her blue-black hair,
   And robed in the rarest Venetian laces,
She moves through her garden frail and fair,
   As one of the plants in those porcelain vases.

Has she a heart? And of what is it made?
   Is she a creature of earth, quite human?
Is she a flower that, placed in the shade,
   Would droop and die? Or is she a woman?

I have studied the question and cannot tell,
   Whether I really dare to love her,
Or whether I might not worship as well
   One of the blue clouds sailing above her.

What if I won her? I would not dare
   To clasp the wonderful myth to my bosom,

In her dainty jewels, and laces rare ;
  'Twould be like crushing some sensitive blossom.

Fair to see as a work of art,
  I could gaze forever upon her beauty ;
But could she love with a woman's heart?
  And perform a wife and mother's duty?

How could a creature so daintily dressed,
  And knowing no thought but her own sweet pleasure,
Nourish a child from her lace-hung breast,
  And yield her youth to a household treasure?

Nay, nay! my lady keep your grace,
  Live and reign in your world of fashion,
And I will find me a plainer face,
  And a heart that has room for love and passion.

MISCELLANEOUS.

THE BELLE OF THE SEASON.

Nay, do not bring me the jewels ;
   Away with that robe of white ;
I am sick of the ball-room, sister,
   I would rather stay here to-night.
"The grandest ball of the season?"
"The upper ten thousands' shout?"
Yes! yes! I know it, my darling,
But I do not care to go.

Last night I was thinking deeply,
   Something I seldom do ;
You know I came home at midnight ;
   Well, I lay awake till two.
I was thinking about my girlhood,
Just how I have spent its years,
And I blushed for shame, my darling,
   And my pillow was wet with tears.

I have lived in a whirl of fashion,
   I have kept right up to the style,
I have learned how to dance the German,
   How to bow, and flirt, and smile.
I have worn most beautiful dresses,
   Been the belle of many a ball,

MISCELLANEOUS.

I have won the envy of women,
   And the praise of fops—that's all.

Does any one really respect me?
   Could a single thing be said
That would give the mourners pleasure,
   To-morrow, if I were dead?
"She wore such beautiful dresses,"
   "She'd a dozen strings to her bow,"
"She could waltz like a perfect fairy,"
   Would you like me remembered so?

Well, there's nothing else to remember.
   What thing have I ever done
That has made a soul the better
   Or cheered a hopeless one?
I have spent my time and money,
   The best of my fortune and days,
In gaining the envy of women,
   And making the poor fops gaze.

I am going to be a woman,
   And live for others, awhile,
Forgetting myself for a season,
   Though I know it isn't the style.
I am in no mood for the revel;
   Away with that robe of white,
And I will stay here my darling,
   And talk with my heart, to-night.

THREE AND ONE.

They stray through the sunlit summery weather,
  Two maids and a youth, 'neath skies of blue,
And each of the three as they walk together,
  Is secretly wishing there were but two.

Yet the maidens love each other dearly,
  And both love the youth, if he only knew,
And he loves one as a sweet friend only,
  And the other he loves as lovers do.

And she who is given his heart's best passion,
  Gives back but a fancy, a passing whim,
She loves him only in coquette fashion,
  While the other maid—she would die for him.

And while they wander across the meadows,
  Their three hearts brimming with love's sweet pain,
Fate is sitting back in the shadows,
  Weaving for them a tangled skein.

And she shall weave till the Autumn weather,
  When the threads shall unravel and all come straight;
But well she loveth to knot them together,
  And tangle the ends for a time, doth Fate.

She at whose feet is cast that treasure,
 A man's heart, strong with love's full tide,
Shall use it awhile, as a thing of pleasure,
 Bruise it and break it, and cast it aside.

And she who is loved as a sweet friend only,
 Shall find it bleeding upon the ground,
And being herself so sad and lonely,
 Shall strive through pity to heal the wound.

And after a time when she's hushed its grieving,
 She shall take it, with all its wounds and scars,
And hide it away in her breast, believing
 'Tis the richest treasure under the stars.

But the three walk o'er the sunlit meadows,
 And dream all life is a summer land,
And they pass by One who sits in the shadows,
 And see not the web in her bony hands.

And so we all, while the days are flitting,
 Plan out a future of joys and pains,
And see not Fate in the shadows sitting,
 Knotting and tying her tangled skeins.

The vows we vow, with a fond "forever,"
 The pledge we deem there can naught befall,

Fate with a touch of her hand can sever;
  Ah me! it is folly to plan at all.

Those we love may the soonest fail us,
  We may learn to worship whom now we hate?
And what do our plans and our dreams avail us?
  Better to leave it all with Fate.

THROUGH TEARS.

An artist toiled over his pictures;
  He labored by night and by day.
He struggled for glory and honor,
  But the world,—it had nothing to say.
His walls were ablaze with the splendors
  We see in the beautiful skies;
But the world beheld only the colors
  That were made out of chemical dyes.

Time sped. And he lived, loved and suffered;
  He passed through the valley of grief.
Again he toiled over his canvas,
  Since in labor alone was relief.
It showed not the splendor of colors
  Of those of his earlier years,
But the world—the world bowed down before it,
  Because it was painted with tears.

A poet was gifted with genius,
   And he sang, and he sang all the days,
He wrote for the praise of the people,
   But the people accorded no praise.
Oh, his songs were as blithe as the morning,
   As sweet as the music of birds;
But the world had no homage to offer
   Because they were nothing but words.

Time sped. And the poet through sorrow
   Became like his suffering kind.
Again he toiled over his poems
   To lighten the grief of his mind.
They were not so flowing and rhythmic
   As those of his earlier years,
But the world—lo! it offered its homage,
   Because they were written in tears.

So ever the price must be given
   By those seeking glory in art;
So ever the world is repaying
   The grief-stricken, suffering heart.
The happy must ever be humble;
   Ambition must wait for the years,
Ere hoping to win the approval
   Of a world that looks on through its tears.

MYSELF.

I was not meant for this cold land.
I am a part, of some far foreign clime,
Where gorgeous-plumaged birds do flit
Among the tropic blooms, or sit
And drink the sun, and pour it out in songs.
There, there my soul belongs.
By some pre-natal error, I became
A dweller here, and shall be for all time.
So I have taught my heart to understand
And bear with this land's moods of ice of snow.
Yet me it doth not know.
And when my soul athirst for warmth and light
Sets my ripe Southern nature all aflame,
The bleak wind seems to howl out words of blame,
Because I do not revel in its night
Of endless winter, but am all aglow
With life and color.—Me it doth not know.
I am not like the people of this land.
They are so pale, so stately and so cold.
They are made out of snow, and I of fire.
They know no intense longing or desire.
Yet I have taught my heart to understand
Their little feelings : and have tuned my lyre
And sung their songs for them : and told
Their woes and sorrows, so they seemed my own—
While foreign to all I have felt or known.
And yet among them all, there is no man,

And not one woman, who knows me; or can
Make least allowance, if for one small hour
My heart blooms out like some great tropic flower—
Ignores their dull, pale, soulless hues, and speaks
Its orient thoughts and feelings on my cheeks.
I live not like the people of this land.
They live for gold, for narrow aims, for fashion,
They hate, they envy, and they dwell in strife.
My soul is steeped in color and in passion.
I love all incense, beauty, light, and heat;
Without them life to me is incomplete.
I am so full of love I cannot hate,
But I love not those forms and airs of state.
Yet I have taught my heart to understand
These ways and manners, to adopt this life
In all externals lest I do displease.
But let me vary from their narrow laws
One least iota, and not one of these
Can overlook it. Like so many daws
They pick at me in anger and dismay.
I understand and pity them, but they
Can never comprehend me.
      Be it so!
But had I wings, how swiftly I would go
To that far island, where I do belong,
And pour my soul out in impassioned song,
And stretch my limbs in freedom 'neath the trees,
And listen to the ever lulling breeze,
And revel in the seas of gorgeous bloom,
My couch in life, in death my peaceful tomb.

This book should be returned to the Library on or before the last date stamped below.

A fine of five cents a day is incurred by retaining it beyond the specified time.

Please return promptly.

CANCELLED

NOV 2 1 1922

DEC 14 1982

763 98 33

Check Out More Titles From HardPress Classics Series In this collection we are offering thousands of classic and hard to find books. This series spans a vast array of subjects – so you are bound to find something of interest to enjoy reading and learning about.

Subjects:
Architecture
Art
Biography & Autobiography
Body, Mind &Spirit
Children & Young Adult
Dramas
Education
Fiction
History
Language Arts & Disciplines
Law
Literary Collections
Music
Poetry
Psychology
Science
…and many more.

Visit us at www.hardpress.net

Im The Story
personalised classic books

"Beautiful gift... lovely finish. My Niece loves it, so precious!"

Helen R Brumfielden

★★★★★

UNIQUE GIFT

FOR KIDS, PARTNERS AND FRIENDS

Timeless books such as:

 Kids

Alice in Wonderland · The Jungle Book · The Wonderful Wizard of Oz
Peter and Wendy · Robin Hood · The Prince and The Pauper
The Railway Children · Treasure Island · A Christmas Carol

 Adults

Romeo and Juliet · Dracula

- **Highly** Customisable
- **Change** Books Title
- **Replace** Characters names with yours
- **Upload** Photos for inside pages
- **Add** inscriptions

Visit **Im The Story**.com
and order yours today!

CPSIA information can be obtained
at www.ICGtesting.com
Printed in the USA
BVHW060220280819
556849BV00020B/3999/P